WINGS OVER THE SOMME
1916-1918

WINGS
over the
SOMME
1916~1918

Wing Commander
Gwilym H. Lewis, DFC

Edited by
Chaz Bowyer

WILLIAM KIMBER · LONDON

First published in 1976 by
WILLIAM KIMBER & CO. LIMITED
Godolphin House, 22a Queen Anne's Gate,
London, SW1H 9AE

ISBN 0 7183 0324 5

Filmset by
Specialised Offset Services Ltd, Liverpool
and printed in Great Britain by
R. J. Acford Limited, Chichester, Sussex

Contents

List of Illustrations

A map of the aerodromes of the Western Front appears on pages 48-9.

To my Father, and my brother Edmund,
my cousin Alan, and my other wonderful
flying comrades of World War One.

Foreword

It was during the course of private research on 1914-18 aviation that I first had the privilege of meeting Wing Commander Gwilym Lewis, the author of the letters which provide the main narrative of this book. A casual reference to the letters by him excited my curiosity initially, but after being permitted to read a random selection I became convinced that such a unique record of the author's youth and times should, indeed must be placed on public record for future historians. These letters, in my view at least, are wholly representative of a generation and a period in British history which is rapidly fading from memory, and one which should be comprehensively recorded for posterity.

To appreciate the content fully it should be recognised that these letters were written at a time of momentous events, by a boy of 18 (initially) hardly out of school, whose academic education and inherited national characteristic of reticence – a strong contemporary mode of deliberate understatement – were by no means uncommon of that era. It was a period in British history when patriotism was a meaningful emotion; duty was a natural conviction of growing manhood; honesty of purpose and high moral judgement perfectly natural facets of that generation's attitude to fellow men. It is a sad commentary indeed on that much-abused description of today's higher education – 'progress' – that a large proportion of the most modern generation of young men find such standards hard to wholly comprehend. During the so-termed 'Great War' of 1914-18 love of country, duty to family, and service to the Monarch were unspoken aims for the nation's youth – Gwilym Lewis, as a young man revealing his thoughts and opinions in these letters to his family, stands as merely one individual, yet exemplifies his generation.

The original letters, preserved so carefully by the author's father, are part of the Lewis family private archives today. In preparing these, or rather a selection of the total, for publication, nothing whatsoever has been altered from its original phrasing or punctuation. Each is quoted verbatim from its original. However, certain sentences, references, and occasionally a paragraph or two have been simply omitted. Such omissions concerned family intimacies, of interest and importance only to the family, and therefore wholly private. Their withdrawal in no way disturbs the flow of the main letter text, nor does it detract from the more directly relevant theme of flying and fighting – the main context intended for the book.

In assembling the text the letters have been deliberately divided into two main sections. This was done not simply for chronological reasons but to illustrate how, with the passing of time and an accumulation of hard-won experience, the author's outlook matured swiftly in the crucible of war. The discerning reader will find a distinct, though entirely unconscious change in opinions and attitude to work and duties by the author. This transition from adolescence to manhood took place within less than two years – the equivalent of several lifetimes in the precarious existence of an operational fighting pilot during the world's first-ever war in the sky.

The overall picture painted by the contents is not one of glory and dashing air combat between 'glamorous' fighting 'aces' – a view of 1914-18 aviation which has been endlessly over-emphasised and publicised in the past. Rather it portrays the day to day feelings, opinions, events of a fighting pilot's existence in those grim years. The author was in fact an 'ace', scoring a credited total of 12 victories and being awarded a Distinguished Flying Cross for his prowess and leadership. Yet the bulk of his letters refer to the dawn to dusk 'routine' matters which occupied perhaps ninety per cent of a pilot's life of that period – the 'daily round' on an RFC squadron in France sixty years ago. Part of that 'routine' was the almost unbearable need to 'adjust' to the deaths of close friends and acquaintances. Only those who have experienced the extraordinary comradeship of a close-knit fighting community, exemplified by a fighter squadron, can fully appreciate the shattering effect of such losses on a young man's mind and outlook.

A majority of the photographs used in illustrations came from Wing Commander Lewis's private albums. For his expert preparation of prints suitable for reproduction, and most generous aid in many other ways, I am indebted to Barrington J. Gray. Further invaluable help with historical data was willingly afforded by a close friend and research colleague, Norman L.R. Franks. The gratitude of all aviation historians should undoubtedly be offered to the publisher, William Kimber, for undertaking the publication of these letters; a special word of thanks being owed to Amy Howlett of that firm for her faith and direct support of the project.

Chaz Bowyer

Norwich, 1976

Captain Gwilym Hugh Lewis, DFC, 1918

Author's Introduction

It must indeed be a fantasy, after all these years, for me to attempt to recreate this story of a period gone by, some of it into history. Throughout those years the most impressionable period for me still remaining is that of the first war, 1914-18, oftimes referred to as the 'Great War'. Obviously, memories of the past, lying forgotten in a cupboard, become tarnished; when looked at again only a few gleams shine out from a pattern that was once so vivid. If it had not been for the enthusiasm of my friend, Chaz Bowyer, himself a lifelong researcher and writer of the period, that cupboard is where these dulled but exciting memories would remain. It so happened that my father preserved the rather school-boyish letters I wrote from France of my time in the air during the great Somme battles of 1916-1918, and it was at these that Chaz glanced and insisted that, being authentic and unadorned, they were of great value as a story of those days.

At the risk of being courtmartialled, I carried a small camera, and am thus able to embellish the narrative with photographs of individual pilots. But it is the letters which are the main focus of interest. Had I known they would have been used in this way, they could have been greatly improved, although for me they still provide some understandable stimulation. I can only hope this may be shared in some degree by my readers. One reason why the saga in my letters could have been of more general interest was that I was very much governed then by the public school boy's attitude of understatement. I learnt in later years, in dealing with enthusiasts like Americans, what a futile quality this could be. My combat reports too were couched in such terms and were incredibly uninteresting.

Looking back to those days, the 'dogfights' were wildly exciting. True, I became a skilled pilot, and my thinking was electric, but oftimes no confirmed results were established in such hectic encounters, and the 'Huns' were driven down to their own territory. On many occasions I recall out-manoeuvring my black-crossed opponent, but shooting had to be short and vital. The deflection could be incredibly difficult, and this I judge is where I fell down. The easy shot on the tail of a diving Hun was a very different matter. Indeed, to an extent I suffered from a somewhat similar handicap in my pheasant or wild fowl shooting of later years. When it came to writing my combat report, it might read, 'Flight engaged 10 EA over Cambrai' – after which, as likely as not, I would fling myself exhausted on my bed to go completely 'out' for a couple of hours. Perhaps I was a bit young?

Later the letters are pitched in a lowish key in consideration of my father. He had plenty of guts and was a leader in the rough and tumble of commerce, but highly sensitive. After my brother Edmund was killed on father's birthday, Boxing Day, 1916, he badly felt the strain when I continued overseas, and in fact suffered a breakdown. Indeed this was a shocking problem for a close-knit family. Another factor was that during periods of concentrated activity, such as September 15th 1916 and subsequent days, when our tanks first went into action, events over-ran letter writing, and the hectic flying excitements of one day to another were soon forgotten.

One aspect which has greatly impressed me during the assembly of this book has been my astonishment at the great interest that now exists in World War I flying. This came as a complete surprise to me. Soon after the armistice of November 1918 I was demobilised and turned to a new and what has been a very active life. Most of my friends were killed, or had returned to the Colonies, and with the exception of those wonderful and stimulating annual dinners at the RAF's Central Flying School, I retained only slender contacts. Even my service in World War 2 was part of an entirely different war.

Recently, with more time on my hands, I encountered the *Cross & Cockade* Society, a group of comparatively young men who, in their spare time, have thoroughly researched the activities of WW1 squadrons, their aircraft and personnel. For example, when it was found that I was an original DH2 pilot, quickly I was subjected to a cross-questioning on the flying capabilities and difficulties of the aircraft, the layout of its cockpit and instrument arrangement, the engine, the Lewis gun, and a host of other details. These men are surprisingly well informed, even to the names of the pilots, squadron records, casualties – indeed, the lot.

About the Author

Gwilym Hugh Lewis was born at Birmingham on 5 August 1897, one of three brothers and three sisters. Educated principally at Marlborough College, he volunteered to join Northampton Regiment TF and was gazetted as Second Lieutenant with effect from 10 September 1915. He soon applied to transfer to the Royal Flying Corps, but the intake was 'full up' and he was advised first to obtain a 'ticket' (flying certificate) at one of the many civilian flying instructional schools. Accordingly he enrolled in the London and Provincial School at Hendon aerodrome, paying a fee of £100 for the privilege. After an accumulated total of some four hours primitive 'instruction' with no dual control on such under-powered school machines as 35 hp and 45 hp Anzani-engined Caudrons, he was awarded his certificate on 27 November 1915. Accepted by the RFC for further flying instruction, Lewis was posted to South Farnborough on 3 January 1916 for a basic course of instruction in ground and air subjects, and on 7 February was sent to Upavon, home of the RFC's Central Flying School – the doyen of all military flying instruction in the world's air services. After advanced flying experience here, Lewis was finally awarded his pilot's brevet ('wings') on 23 April 1916.

From Upavon, Lewis joined 32 Squadron RFC, then in the process of its original formation at Netheravon. Eventually equipped throughout with the De Havilland 2 Scout, 32's first commander was another Welshman, Major Lionel Rees, MC, a regular Army officer who had already seen wide active service in France as a pilot with 11 Squadron RFC, and been awarded a Military Cross for his prowess. On 29 May 1916, 32 Squadron flew to France for operations, arriving on the front at a period when the German Air Service was gaining a measure of supremacy in the aerial conflict, and the First Battle of the Somme broke out on 1st July. Along with its sister DH2 unit, 24 Squadron, the unit quickly began to establish a fine fighting reputation – exemplified, perhaps, by the courageous single-handed fight against great odds by its commander, Lionel Rees, on 1 July (detailed in the author's contemporary letters), which resulted in the award of a Victoria Cross to Rees.

For the next six months after arrival in France, Lewis, though at 18 the youngest member of 32 Squadron, gained invaluable fighting experience, and indeed accounted for at least three enemy aircraft in combat, before being sent to England for an appendectomy operation. Once fully fit again, Lewis was posted to Loch Doon in Ayrshire on 10 February 1917, as an instructor on the newly-forming school of aerial fighting at Camlarg. In June he was further posted, as an instructor at the CFS, Upavon, and promoted to Captain with effect from 10 September 1917. At Upavon Lewis was given command of the SE5 Flight; training fighter pilots for France. It was experience which was to stand him in good stead when, on 9 December 1917, he was posted back to France, as a Flight commander with one of the most distinguished fighter squadrons of the RFC, No.40, flying SE5s and SE5As.

For the following eight months, Lewis led his Flight over the Western Front, flying and fighting almost daily; alongside such redoubtable fighters as 'Mick' Mannock, Roderic Dallas, George McElroy, L.A. Herbert, Tudhope, and many others, through some of the fiercest air fighting of the war. His qualities as both a fighter, and especially a leader, are possibly best exemplified by the fact that he never lost a single novice pilot from his Flight in combat. Indeed, contrary to the usual contemporary practice of having a 'new boy' at the rear of any fighting formation, Lewis always placed a 'novice' next to him in the leading section, usually flanked by another experienced pilot, for protection until the novitiate had gained sufficient fighting experience. By August 1918, though unaware of it personally, Lewis had virtually reached his peak of fighting efficiency. The award of a Distinguished Flying Cross thus marked official recognition of his personal prowess, but emphasised his outstanding value as a fighting leader.

The final months of 1918 were spent, again, as an instructor at CFS, Upavon. Despite his original reactions to his first period of service at Upavon (see letters), the Central Flying School had become virtually a second home to Lewis; he had an affection for the unit which has continued to this day.

Deciding against a permanent career in the post-1918 Royal Air Force, Gwilym Lewis was demobilised on 28 January 1919, and the next day began a career in commerce; some details of which are contained in the final chapter of this book. The finale to his long World War I flying career is best summed up in Gwilym Lewis's own words, 'In a sort of way this was a sad parting for me, but already my mind was searching in other skies. I had just loved my flying before all else – the feeling of bird-like gracefulness and perfection meant much to me – but I had already found that even with two or three weeks off I had lost a little of that sensitive or perfect flying touch. I concluded that, as several years had gone by since I had left school, there were a great many things I had not done, or missed the opportunity to do. So I decided not to touch the 'joystick' again – and I never have.'

PART I

1916

Royal Flying Corps School
South Farnborough
16 January 1916

My dearest Mother and Father,
It seems quite like school again to have to send home sort of reports
on progress. Ah! those were good times when I used to scratch my
head to see if it would not assist me in any way to reach the bottom of
the last side of a sheet of notepaper, and when that method failed, as
it invariably did, I always had to send for a special boy, and hear all
the information that *he* had put in *his* letters, and if I thought it was
good down it went into mine. The wretched boy used to go half
through his family history to me sometimes.

Well, to get to business, I suppose you will not be greatly surprised
to hear I have done a little wandering in the air. My first flight I went
up in an Avro with dual control. I got as far as taking the controls
after about 1000 feet which was quite simple on that occasion. When
things seemed to be a bit slow my pilot, Lt Ward, also Flight
Commander, did some vertical turns etc to liven things up. The chief
thing I noticed was how completely I lost my direction in the air; I
hadn't a ghost of an idea where I was in relation to the aerodrome,
and my chief thought was 'Good Heavens, what am I going to do
when I go cross-country.' However, the aerodrome suddenly loomed
into view, and he did the landing. What I learnt was that the Avro
was very sensitive fore and aft, and also on the rudder. However I
imagine it wouldn't take me long to get into after the Box-kite,
though the landing is very much faster.

Well, on Friday they had a rotten old Caudron ready for use, so
up I went in that. It was rather a difficult affair to the old ones at
Hendon, though this particular specimen was less pleasure to fly.
One thing it is fitted with an 80 hp Gnome, and another the wing
span is very much greater. I imagine my Flight Commander has
rather less love for the brute than I have for he sent me right up solo.
I think he must have thought it would it would be a quick way of

The author at Hendon, 1915, during his initial flying instruction.

putting the beast out of action. However after a few minutes deliberation I decided I would not oblige him, I did a couple of straights quite passably. We have a long straight of about ¾ mile long here. After that I was ready to have a look round aloft. So up I started, (it was a beautiful day, though there was a lot of drift) and had a good squint at things. I found various railways; I chased down one and got tired of it, so I followed another in the direction of London. I did a few turns to relieve the monotony, and found I was at 3,500 feet. It slowly dawned on me that it was beastly cold, so I descended to 1500 where it was decidedly better. I followed round the aerodrome and landed without mishap. My only impression was that cross-country flying must be terribly boring on a fine day, and still worse on a windy day.

On Saturday it was said that there was from 50-60 miles of wind aloft, so I didn't go up. On Sunday I spent most of the day waiting for them to get another Caudron into shape, one which is decidedly nicer to fly, and after I had spent the majority of the day waiting, they decided one of the inlet valves had gone. However, I managed to get up in the original Caudron, but as it was rather foggy, I changed my original intention of going cross-country and confined my efforts to the neighbourhood of the aerodrome. I started off in great style with my engine missing, however, it finished missing at about 100 feet, all of which time I was busy with my eyes on the rev counter, and seeing that I didn't climb in too much hurry. These Caudrons climb like smoke.

I contented myself with a maximum height of about 2,000 and occupied my time with doing various turns. I tried some old 'eights' again, and tried to turn a complete circle once or twice. However I was very careful and didn't try vertical banks or anything, though it is best to make good use of these very scanty fine days and try to enjoy one's self.

After I had been up about 40 minutes I came down as it was beginning to get dark. To tell you the truth I find it rather boring to hang about up there for long, though I am always fairly well awake. As I was meditating an engine failure while over Aldershot, it struck me that houses certainly ought to be abolished. They are made so horribly hard, aren't they? I am not anxious for my first forced landing! That's all the flying I have done.

The fellows down here are a very good lot. A large number of them are regulars who have come from Sandhurst, and as a whole the

The Royal Aero Club Certificates – pilot's civilian 'tickets' – issued to the author (top) and his father. Hugh Lewis (senior), who at the age of 50, learned to fly in the winter of 1915 at the Grahame White School at Hendon.

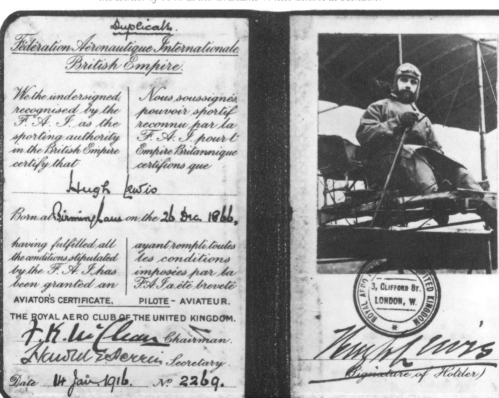

social standard I should imagine is pretty good. Of course, a large number of them are a bit lively, but what can you expect from flying men. I was always slow to make friends, and consequently haven't done very much down here yet, though there are some awfully good men about.

South Farnborough, 19 January 1916
The expected news (*see p.26*) has just reached me, and I offer my heartiest congratulations. There is not the slightest doubt you have accomplished something very fine, and I am sure not one man in ten thousand would have attempted what you have accomplished, if they had been in your position. I wish you had handed down a little bit more of your pluck. Now don't get very rash and start doing wonderful stunts. We are all liable to crashes, even the youngest of us, and the large majority of them are caused through the irresistible attraction of trying to be clever. My great ambition is to do some stunts, though at present I am going easy. Besides I can get up to about 4000 without much difficulty and a little patience.

I have had an hour and three-quarters last week. Not so much as I might have had. One time I got quite smothered in clouds at 1,000 feet. It's a nasty feeling, even if only momentary. Caudrons are hated like poison down here. I don't hate them myself though they are very inefficient flying machines. However, they climb like smoke, and come down like lead. A fellow has crashed the Caudron I was flying to bits, so that is one out of the way. Another one is nearly ready, quite a good one I believe, and meanwhile I am doing some dual control on an Avro. I hope I shall soon get into that and go solo. Some of the fellows go up here when you have to hold your hat on your head. Of course I don't, and don't want to do so on a Caudron, but it is a good squadron in that way. However, it's not nice if one's engine goes to sleep. I haven't done a proper cross-country yet. I should rather like to do one. I'd like to fly over to Hendon and have a race with you. I am awfully pleased you have accomplished the great trick at last. The fellows make quite a fuss of it down here. I get quite tired of hearing about their first solos on Longhorns etc. The Hendon people don't make half the fuss.

Central Flying School, Upavon, Pewsey, Wiltshire. 9 February 1916
I am fairly in for it now. I have arrived at the one spot that every RFC man prays he shall never go to, and although I didn't pray

quite as hard as some, I did my bit. Five of us came over together and there were a number of Farnborough people over here before, so between us all there has been a fair amount of bad language used. The thing that upset us more than anything else was that it was nine miles away from a railway station, and right out on Salisbury Plain, the most horribly cold spot on earth. However, it is the principal flying school in England and I have heard it said that it is the best in the world, so I suppose there are two sides to the question. Nevertheless it is one of those places where the wind blows a gale, the rain comes down in sheets, and the sun shines like fury, all at the same time!

The discipline down here is very strict which of course is very annoying, and also a little dangerous with flying men, as their work is so very individual. They also have a nasty habit of firing you out if you crash, especially if they take a dislike to you, so I am prepared for all eventualities. If that had been the rule at Farnborough I fear my number would have been up as I crashed two machines in one effort. I was on an Avro and overshot my landing a bit and had to turn down 'straight' which was against the rules. Just as I had finished my landing a Longhorn came swooping down, and had just touched the ground before either of us noticed one another. However, the pilot yanked her up again without putting his engine on in an endeavour to jump me, as we should have crashed horribly, centre to centre otherwise. He caught his undercarriage in my top plane, crashing the Longhorn to matchwood. It was my fault because I was more advanced and should have kept a lookout, and also because I landed on the wrong side of the 'straight'.

Down here I have got into a horrible Flight with 'Bloaters' and Martinsyde Scouts. 'Bloaters' is another name for BE8, which is a sort of BE with a Gnome engine. It is an old freak and a failure, so I suppose that is why we are given it to fly. It certainly is a most horrible object. Absolutely unstable, wheel control and warp wings. Everyone is very terrified of it, and it is supposed to spin at the slightest provocation, and once in a spin, Lord help you! I imagine great care has to be taken with turning, not to put too much rudder or too little bank. So far I have only been up dual control, and find it very difficult to land well. The landing ground here is very level and shows all bumps. However, I suppose I have got to fly these rotten things, so I am going to go on grumbling. I haven't stopped since I came here.

'Huns' – the soubriquet used in the RFC to denote pilots under instruction. An informal snap of the author (right) with A.M. Windsor (left) and 'Teddy' Holstius (seated centre), at the Central Flying School, Upavon, 1916. The author was later best man at Holstius' wedding.

They have the best of most things down here, and we get very good lectures, better than before. There are very few BE2c and such things here. They are mostly old freaks like BE2a, BE2b, BE8 and BE8a. I should love to get on an Avro or BE2c again. The quarters are old wooden huts and not so bad; the messing is quite good, but has to be paid for, and the ante room is a perfect joke. The hours are worse than ever, and on the whole I suppose it is a very fine school, though I am now praying that I shall not pass straight out from this solitary confinement to the Front, but get a short time with some other squadron in England, Croydon for choice.

Central Flying School, Upavon, Wilts. 12 March 1916
Last week has been most uneventful. Quite the most important occurrences have been the receiving of a large number of good things

from home. Bar that, the most important episode has been going out to tea with my Flight commander. The whole Flight were there but the importance is that I saved 6d by having tea out of Mess! He is a most excellent fellow and a jolly good Flight commander. He is the second I have had since I've been here, and both have been awfully good fellows and seen considerable service in France, and strange to say they are both most considerate fellows who think before they send you up, if you are a bit of a beginner. H.R. Nichols, my present Flight commander, has been gold mining in Rhodesia for a good many years, and I must say I would rather be on his side in a street fight if there was any choice.

I have been on a workshop course last week, and so I had about half an hour's flying. It is extraordinary how one's opinions will change. I actually am glad I am flying 'Bloaters' now instead of BE2c's for the simple reason that you have to *fly* them, and very properly too, while BE2c's being stable are apt to fly you, and don't get into trouble easily. I cannot say I have got to the stage where I actually enjoy flying these 'Bloaters', but I am pretty certain that finally I shall know much more about flying than a BE2c man whose 'bank' comes on automatically by applying rudder.

On the other hand 'Bloaters' are quite unstable and keep you in a sort of panic on a windy day, and one is frightened at being up, and still more scared of coming down. The great drawback is the Gnome engine which I quite detest. However, I am getting used to it, and can tell more or less how I am flying without bothering with my instruments. I can more or less tell by the sound whether I have the nose down or whether I am stalling. I nearly stalled the other day when I was having a look round the country on a turn, but I detected it by the sound of the engine and got the nose down in good time.

Of course, you always lose a good deal of speed on a turn, and it is always safest to dip your nose slightly before a turn as there is less chance of spinning if you have plenty of speed. I am afraid I very seldom do it as I always try to turn perfectly level. If you are turning from up-wind to down-wind you certainly should hold your nose down a bit, especially if the wind is moderately strong. The reason is, of course, that while turning down-wind your relative ground speed increases, it is some time before your wind speed is the same as it was going up-wind. It is easy to see this by taking your ground speeds. If your machine speed is 60 mph and there is a 30 mph wind, going against the wind your pace is 60-minus-30, while with the wind it is

60-plus-30. A difference of 60 mph which has all to be obtained on the turn, to prevent stalling.

I have to thank Mother very much for the mitts, they are fine. The muffler has been of the greatest value and is inestimable while flying. I have also received an excellent cake and some sweets. Reminds me of Farnborough when I always kept some chocolates in store. I have dipped well into *The First Hundred Thousand*. It is a first rate book, and awfully popular. There are about six copies here, and everyone is shouting, 'After you'. It is very funny and everything is so absolutely true. It is a book everyone should read.

Central Flying School, Upavon, Wilts. 30 March 1916
I am afraid I have some requests to make. I have hesitated long before making them because I know how busy you must be with the new dwelling place, but any time within a week or even a fortnight will do. My trouble is that things might take a very sudden turn for me now, and I might be whisked overseas at a moment's notice, though I don't expect it will happen before about a month. I am in need of some woollens, and I fear only the best will suit me. I usually swear by Jaeger's. First of all, I want a warm woollen cardigan waistcoat with long sleeves, then a Balaclava hat to come over my head, moderately long in the neck and very warm, please! I take about size 7 in hats. Then I want some thick socks as all my present ones are 'wash-outs'. I should like six pairs to fit size 9 boots, and three to fit size 10 boot. If when you settle down you find my yellow khaki collars or shirts I should very much like to have them; they are not at all important though.

I did my second trip on a BE2c yesterday, and went up to about 6,000, and amongst other places circled round Salisbury. On my way home I looped. It was quite nice, but took more will power than I should like to exert often. I am pleased to think I am the first one down here to do it without wings, and there are only about two who have done it with wings who are under instruction. It was a beautifully clear day and I could see for miles from that height; I looked hard for Stonehenge but I am not sure I saw it. In the afternoon I went to Devizes, and in the evening I went over Marlborough and came down to about 1,000 ft but I didn't see anyone around so I didn't risk a landing. This morning I went to Andover, but it wasn't nice as the clouds kept getting in the way and it started to rain, and I can tell you it stings one's face up some.

The things I want, tabulated, are -
1 Cardigan
9 Socks (6 of sz 9 & 3 of sz 10)
1 Balaclava
1 Thick undervest
1 Thick pants

Central Flying School, Upavon, Wilts. 6 April 1916

I have had rather a bit of bad luck this week; I found on returning that I cannot get my wings for some time yet as I come under the new system I was telling you about. The only way it affects me is financially, which is probably the worst. Amongst the various items on the programme are the following; we must do at least 15 hours on a Service machine. These are the machines they fly at the Front; I haven't flown one yet. Land on a circle of 50 paces radius from 6,000 feet. I managed to do this, though it was an awful struggle. Do a cross-country of not less than 60 miles, landing twice on strange spots, and flying at 6,000. Night flying officers who have graduated are to be encouraged to fly in every kind of bad weather. Fellows who have just got their wings have got to do this too, and I only missed mine by one day; my name has been sent up. It is rather an amusing programme.

I have done nearly eight hours flying already this week, and I suppose there is plenty more to come. People who have had one joy ride on a calm day cannot imagine anyone having too much of this business, but already there are cases of fellows going 'dud' and being given a week's leave because they never get a rest. Of course, there is nothing much wrong in running around in a BE2c unless it is bumpy, but it is when you are in a strange machine that one's nerves get a bit on edge, especially if it is a very fast one.

Tomorrow, or very shortly, I expect to fly an FE, or what is known down here as the 'Flying Commode' or 'Flying Coffin'. They are huge things. I expect Father will remember one being down at Hendon one Sunday long ago. I expect they will put the wind up me landing, as they have to be landed very slowly or else they run for miles (they weigh over a ton) and they glide without ceasing. I find it bad enough to get a BE2c into the aerodrome but what it will be like with these things I cannot think. The number of taps, gauges, pumps and instruments that have to be seen to are enough to make anyone crazy. They are fitted with 120 hp Austro-Daimler engines. No dual control this time either.

I expect Father will remember A.B. de Brandon,[1] the Zeppstrafer at Hendon. He was the fellow who got lost while taking his ticket and made a successful landing outside the aerodrome. I have met him since, just after he got his wings.

Central Flying School, Upavon, Wilts. 16 April 1916

I see that Mr Grey of the *Aeroplane* says that last week's show at Hendon was one of the finest since the outbreak of war, so I think I was very lucky. *He* is one of the people who greatly annoy me now; he *thinks* he knows such a lot about the Services. He also talks about 'water-cooled' Lewis machine guns.[2]

Of course quite the most important thing is that Edmund has rolled up here, as you probably have heard. He will go into a Longhorn Flight under an ex-Flight commander of mine; a most excellent fellow. He has had very bad luck in being put into a tent, but he will be able to use my room during the day. A crowd of other people have come down too from various places and they have been planted in tents. We have had some very bad weather this week in the way of high winds and rain, so flying has almost been suspended, which is very aggravating.

On returning here at the beginning of the week I found I had been transferred to a Vickers Gunbus and De Havilland Scout Flight. My present object therefore is to fly a Vickers. At present I have been up for a 15-minute joy ride on one, and since then the weather has been too rotten to take one up. I have gone past the stage when I get any more dual control, and it will be my first proper attempt at flying a pusher. A great 100 hp Monosoupape sits behind me and makes an awful row. I believe they are ripping to fly; simply turn corners like a scout, but they do not glide very well, and the landing will be rather interesting at first. The DH2 Scout comes later, and if I survive this I *might* fly an FE8, which is very similar but faster; topping things I believe. However, it does not do to look too far ahead as I might change Flights several times before then.

Central Flying School, Upavon, Wilts. 23 April 1916

The last few days we have done quite a heap of work down here. I think I told you I had changed my Flight to fly the Vickers Gunbus. On Thursday the weather cleared up, so I had to take one up. After a few preliminary excitements I managed to get up, having just

The Vickers FB9, an improved version of the FB5 'Gunbus'.

jumped a fence. I stayed up for 35 minutes, as I found the controls very stiff. However, they were quite pleased to see the machine back as they thought I had lost myself, and I was very pleased to find I had landed without killing myself. Since then I have been up continually, and have already amassed nearly 10 hours. I really quite like the old boys. I can turn as sharp as anything on them and spiral rippingly. I pull the stick into me nearly every time and they fairly whizz round. On Friday I gave Marlborough a great entertainment from a height, spiralling round and dodging in and out of clouds. Horrid things clouds! Yesterday I went with another fellow to Farnborough and landed at Netheravon coming back. Extra-ordinary to relate we both got back. It was a horrid journey going there, with a side wind the whole way, and you could only see just below; a black mist hung all round.

I have made three jolly good efforts to kill myself on Vickers but no luck. Each time I swing as I get off and as soon as I can pull the brute off the ground I have to do a right-angled turn about three feet up. I have been ticked off for it once, as I was going straight for a shed, and all the mechanics started tearing away for all they were worth. But I managed to get her off the ground and did a nice bank just off the ground. Personally I rather like them but they seem to put the wind up the onlookers horribly.

I hope soon to fly De Havilland 2 Scouts and then I shall be able to simply buzz round the aerodrome. I see in orders that I have scraped through and got my wings; so that is done with now. I believe Edmund is getting on very well; his Flight commander seemed quite pleased with him, and I think he is very keen on it, though of course everyone has strange sensations at first. I think he finds it a little bit difficult judging his distance from the ground, though that will all come, of course.

RFC Netheravon, Wilts. 9 May 1916

I told you when I was home last that I hoped to be sent to No 32 Squadron. It was the one object for which I had been made to fly DH Scouts, instead of the Martinsyde Scout as had been originally intended. Of course I had grown to look forward to joining the squadron and ever since I had returned from leave I had got terrible wind up that they were going to leave myself and two others out. However, we were sent for yesterday! It is an ideal squadron, and it has been my one ambition to go out with it, but I find we are at present five over strength, so I fear my chances are small being amongst the last joined, and not being a good pilot of the brute (DH2) having never had enough practice. They hope to go out on the 17th which I think is doubtful, and as I have not been told yet to the contrary, I am prepared to go out with them.

Major L.W.B. Rees is in command and it is he who makes the squadron mostly ideal. He has got permission to go out as a flying squadron commander, and he can teach every member of his squadron how to fly. He has published a booklet on how to rig the DH2 and was this evening giving a lecture on the Mono engine. He knows his job thoroughly and above all is a perfect gentleman. I shouldn't be surprised if he comes home with a VC; he has already got an MC. Half the reason why I am keen to go out with him is because I know several of the fellows well; however, I feel the chances are remote.

I had a little excitement the day after I arrived back from leave. I was flying the DH2 in the early morning when I got into a spinning nose dive resulting from a left-hand turn. I was as near as I have been to the 'bone orchard' as yet. I started at 3,000 feet & I got out at about 20 ft up; at one time I saw my pitot tube show 120 mph and I thought I was 'for it'. However, after attempting several stunts, I banked into the spin and managed to push my nose down still further; I think I got down in pretty good time, not more than 30 seconds I am told. I put my engine on again and flew back, finishing up with quite a good landing. The doctor had arrived and the commandant, who is a terribly fat chap, looked blue in the face. He had *run* a considerable distance to see me, and had instructed my Flight commander to 'strafe' me and then send me on to him, as he thought I was trying some fancy stunt of my own, and had nearly killed *him* in the effort.

It is a good thing we are made so that we keep cool in a show like that. I was perfectly quiet all the way down although I thought it was my last journey, and my one thought when I came out and thought that I should have to land on some stubble was, 'What will my Flight commander say if I land across wind and crash?'. I know another fellow who got into the same mess on a Bristol, and he thought he was 'for it', and was perfectly calm all the time. It was rather extraordinary as I know I would lose my head as soon as anybody at any ordinary show. Now it is over I am very pleased I had the experience, and you will be surprised to hear that the lesson I learnt from it is always climb on your turns! This only applies to the DH2, of course.

RFC Netheravon, Wilts. 26 May 1916
We are fearfully busy down here now, everything has to be in perfect order for Sunday. All our transport has gone, and a very fine sight it was, all lined up. I am pleased to say that I am going to fly across after all; a machine has fallen vacant. Unfortunately she is not flying quite perfectly yet, so I have been working on it till after 10 pm tonight. Officers are given a fitter and rigger to see to their machines, and are absolutely responsible for them themselves. My machine is only a matter of rigging. I hope she will carry me across, though I shouldn't be the first one to come down on such an occasion if she didn't. If the weather is good on Sunday I expect we shall leave about 10 am via Farnborough, following the SECR through Kent, and land at Folkestone. The stop at Folkestone will only be for a few hours we rather suspect.

I am terribly sorry to hear about Basden,[3] especially as we are going out to relieve his very squadron, as they are doing our work. I have heard from Taylor[4] of the same squadron, though he forgot to mention Basden. We are going to give the Huns some trouble when

The author, as a Second Lieutenant RFC, shortly after being awarded his 'wings', 1916.

No 32 Squadron RFC at Netheravon, prior to take off for France 28 May 1916. Under the command of Major L W B Rees, MC (later VC). Back row L to R: Charles Bath, H W von Poellnitz, E Henty, G H Lewis (author), J C Simpson, Nicholas. Next row: Nixon, S P Simpson, O V Thomas. Sitting: Stubbs, Capt G Allen, Capt Gilmour, Major Rees, MC, Capt Hellyer. Front: F H Coleman, Corby, P B G Hunt.

we go out. A Fokker doesn't frighten No.32 (as yet!) Address in France: No.32 Squadron, RFC, BEF, France.

No 32 Squadron, RFC, BEF, France. Wednesday, 31 May 1916
First of all I must thank you for the great send-off I had in writing, letters sprouted from everywhere; letters of good advice (which are, of course, the most important) and letters of cheery farewell. I know I only gave everyone very short notice of my departure, as I think it was best, although I must admit that I had a fairly accurate idea of the date a few days after I started flying Vickers. The original date was the 17th.

I don't *think* I shall ever bring disgrace on my country or name, but if I may say so it is awful 'hot air' all this about my being plucky and so on. I know I shall be scared to death the first time these 'archies' start bursting round me, though I must admit that at present I cannot imagine myself running away from a Hun so long as I have a gun and machine in working order. I think we have rather pity for the Hun Flying Corps in spite of their cunning and wile, though we certainly respect their 'archies', and plenty of practice they get too, much more than ours do![5]

Well, I will tell you what I have done since the day we left. Of course I had a few things to do as my machine was flying slightly right wing down, but that was natural. We started next morning about 11 am and I think 32 left as much an impression on Netheravon as any squadron has. Half an hour was given to get engines tested and generally ready. The whole squadron was lined up and at a given signal all the engines were started up again, and away we went in Flights, 1,2,3,4, then a gap, and then the next Flight. We chased each other up into the air as near as we dared, each Flight rendezvoused over a pre-arranged spot and off we started for Folkestone.

Our Flights were in perfect line for 20 miles right above the clouds. Twelve out of 14 arrived at Folkestone after a jolly long journey. One of the others crashed through engine trouble near Farnborough, and went immediately to get a new machine; the other landed safely with slight engine trouble. Another one wanted a slight repair at Folkestone.

The remainder set off for France after a very good lunch at the Metropole. It was beautifully clear crossing, you could easily see across, yet they were about 10 of the most horrid moments of my life, as there seemed to be no cross-Channel work, and I knew I should come down in some wretched minefield. This was added to by the knowledge that my engine was somewhat uncertain. However, all went well, and I reached my destination safely. Another fellow had engine trouble and just managed to glide onto the sands at Cap Gris Nez. The others have since joined up, and here we are about twenty miles behind the Lines in one of the large towns of N. France* I don't mind telling you that it wasn't considered a bad effort getting across with one crash.

The whole of Monday I spent re-rigging the whole of my machine, as I was not quite satisfied with it. Yesterday we went for a 65 miles joy ride, four of us, to visit a sister squadron, right down on the south part of the Lines. Things are quite different down there to what they are up north, yet they have done exceptionally well. They have gained the genuine article, supremacy of the air. They simply cannot

* St. Omer. See page 41.

find any Huns. If a Hun sees a De Hav he runs for his life; they won't come near them. It was only yesterday that one of the fellows came across a Fokker. The Fokker dived followed by the De Hav but the wretched Fokker dived so hard that when he tried to pull his machine out his elevator broke and he dived into our Lines; not a shot was fired. The archies down there are not nearly so good as they are up north either. From what I have seen archies are rather beasty sort of animals!

Today, amongst other things, we went to see our aerodrome,* now held by No.27. We shall not go there for about ten days after we leave here, as we are going somewhere else first. No.27 is wretched Basden's squadron. I suppose you know he is 'done in'. There is not the slightest doubt that he was from the start, as he came down from 12,000. The Huns were very decent, gave him a jolly good funeral and crowds of people were there. They dropped photos of it later. Our gunners made six direct hits on his machine lying on the ground, so the Huns didn't get much out of it! H.A. Taylor is with the squadron now who was a great chum of mine, and later of Basden's. He is the reckless motor driver. I also know another fellow – at Hendon with me. I am terribly sorry about poor Basden. He was one of the very best of fellows, and he and I and a few others used to go joy-riding into Salisbury etc quite often; he also used to belong to our Pyjamas Club.

The RFC is a most wonderful institution. You are never lost in it. As soon as I arrived here in France there were three people I knew. Every squadron I visit I know two or three, and today I met my old Flight commander of Farnborough, and also the CO with a Morane squadron, and a jolly fine squadron too. We hope to start work on Friday. Our aerodrome is quite nice, but they are all terribly small out here, and not too good. When I arrived over France the size of the field scared me, but I see now it is not so bad as there are no hedges. Every square foot is cultivated.

I must say I think France is a bit of a 'hole'. We are now at the best hotel in town, billetted; but except for the food and a comfortable bed it isn't 'in' with a comfortable inn at home. It is purely an eating house. Nasty and untidy, kitchen chairs and tables lying about in a mucky looking room with two funny looking wash basins in the corner. The streets are nasty and dirty, and the people have a nasty habit of throwing all their refuse out into the streets to be taken

* Fienvillers.

away. The women seem very slovenly and untidy (and fat and ugly!) and the whole place seems to be sleepy.

I will admit that I never realised there was a war on until I came here. Not a man to be seen. Women, boys and old men are doing all the work in the towns and in the fields. All the carts are driven by women, and nine-tenths of the women are in black. I certainly never realised there was a war on in England. No one does. You can't help it out here. Everything is in khaki or blue. Every town is full of British soldiers either resting or doing work behind the lines. Hospital cars, transport and staff cars crowd the dusty roads. And wonderful roads they are too on the whole; all lined with big trees and good to follow from above.

The whole squadron is in good form. All rather keen on a strafe. We thought we would get some fun the first morning we were here as a Hun was signalled quite close here coming over in this direction. But nothing happened.

No 32 Squadron, 10th Wing, RFC, BEF, France.
Sunday evening, 4 June 1916
I have been in France just one week, yet it has all been so new and interesting that I could swear I have been out here a month. I am only just beginning to realise that there is a war on, a thing that is almost impossible to realise in England and even at twenty miles behind the firing line. Of course I have heard the guns strafing when I have been closer to the Lines and it is apt to get on one's nerves at first, but of course it has no business to. At 11 pm the other night there was quite a shine on at Ypres, and I don't think we·had it all our own way. However, it is a mere nothing in this show.

I have thoroughly enjoyed life out here so far, simply because I have done nothing except just strafe around. Now that we have moved I cannot see that there is any harm in telling you we *were* at St Omer, as it is the spot where everyone reports who comes from England. It used to be a favourite spot for the Huns to bomb, but they never came near when we were there; one was signalled to be coming in our direction the first day we arrived, but he never came, though we had prepåred a good reception for him.

It is really fearfully funny; there does not appear to be a single decent French linguist in the squadron, and I have turned out to be one of the best. You should have seen what a nut I.was at the hotel with the girls. They did not know my name so I was called '*Le Petit*

Noir' from the colour of my hair. Unfortunately, none of them cried when I left, in fact they did nothing but laugh; of course, I put that down to the fact that they knew nothing of my business!

After playing about at St Omer and getting fattened up for the fray for a week, we left for a position further south than where I thought we were going. It is Sunday today and we start work tomorrow; two hour-patrols. A list was brought round and my name was missing, so I cheered heartily; but a quarter of an hour later I was told I was on at 6.30 am – rather a jar! But I suppose it is what I came out for. I have not to cross the Lines, so it will be an awful fluke if I do. However, these archies are brutes. I shall feel an awful ass if I am brought down the first time, shalln't I?

However, it is really a nice soft job as far as the RFC out here goes. The more I see out here the less I agree with Miss R – when she supposes the RFC is a nice soft job as far as jobs in the Army go. Ask fellows who have had a shot at being under shell fire and archies' fire, and see which they would prefer.

You would love to come out here and have a look round. I have visited several squadrons and the size of their aerodromes are perfectly ridiculous. Silly little patches, some of them covered with cinders. The hangars are more or less substantial but my own machine lies in a canvas construction, and as a matter of fact it is in that that I am sitting now (on a tool box, watching my machine being put into perfect trim for the morrow!)

But what would surprise you more is the respect we get out here as a DH squadron. We are really absolutely 'the ones' here. The DH2 has practically scared the Huns off the Front. Occasionally they manage to steal over at about 15,000 but even then they hesitate whether they dive on a DH or not, if he happened to be below them. The FE's complain that they can get no fights hardly now; it is awfully amusing. Of course, the DH's job is to attack and away he goes at any Hun he sees. You must not think that this is an absolute rule but even in the Hun Flying Corps there are a few chaps with a little life, but they are jolly careful how they attack, if they do, and not many of them fight. Personally I am much less scared of attacking a single-seater Fokker than a slower two-seater with a couple of gun mountings. However, I reserve the right to change my opinions once again!!

We created an awfully good impression 'getting off' at St Omer this morning. It is a sight to see a whole squadron take off in succession. Besides, Major Rees is an absolute prince, and gets us a good name himself. Nearly all the RFC in France knows about us being out here now. O, I must tell you a horrid shock I had yesterday. I was strafing about in the neighbourhood of St Omer, at about 9,000, when I saw a machine right away in the distance. I got terrible wind up as I only had one drum (of ammunition), so I thought I had better nose into him, so I fixed my drum on and went shyly for him, of course, terribly scared. I took him side on and nosed round behind him, when I found he was another DH. Needless to say I felt much better! I suppose this sort of thing will happen often. I hope I shall not take it into my head to strafe one of our own machines. Anyhow I shouldn't be the first to do so.

Our first day here has been splendid. I am writing from bed now, and a jolly good bed too. We are situated in a filthy little mining village. Everyone takes a casual interest in us; we are not the first squadron to be here. We mess in two sections. Our section, B and C Flights, mess in a little room seating 12 round the table. Our food consists of rations brought from England, and very nice too. No cooking necessary. We have not started drawing any regular rations yet. Our Ante Room is a little room in the dwelling across the street. Unfortunately it is sadly short of sit-upons! I dwell in a little cottage a few doors down. The old lady of the house is very affable, chattering gaily in French whenever I appear on the horizon, and I answer as I think fit. My room is upstairs in a sort of attic. I sleep in a large, quite comfortable bed for which I have been lucky to obtain sheets. They feel as if they were made of canvas, but they are good enough. Of course there is no wash-stand, but I have rigged a canvas one up, and I have my orderly to call me in the morning. What more can a man want?

I have recently been told that I am not wanted for patrol tomorrow, which rather annoys me, as I had worked myself up to go have a look and come back and tell the fellows all about it, don't you know! However, I suppose I shall get plenty in time.

The wind is horrid tonight and it is raining, so perhaps we shall have an aviators' holiday tomorrow. You have no idea how we love low clouds and rain. Wind and broken clouds count as nothing out here. I am afraid I have been 'hot airing' more than is good for me, and my candle is rotten, and I feel like reposing in slumber. Best love to everyone. I often think of old England, it seems so near by aeroplane. Fellows used to bring machines across every day. Never forget that nothing is ever made public from letters from the Front.

32 Squadron 10th Wing RFC, Friday 9 June 1916
This is really a jolly comic life out here. Here I am sitting in a dirty ditch, on a box of petrol tins, and supposed to be supervising the mess a fellow is making of my engine because it wouldn't take me to the lines this morning. Oh! I was wild with it, poor old thing! I am glad to hear those efforts of Elliot and Fry [photos] turned out moderately well. How those ladies must have admired my photo at your 'at home' day Mum! It is cheery to think someone has found something 'magnificent' about me, even if it is a photo.

A few days ago we left the dirty little coaling village for our original destination. We have been at work for some days now. There has not been much done owing to the bad weather. We flew over here between the showers, and I took ages to find the aerodrome. It is a comic little show, not quite a Hendon though. However, we are glad to be here as we expect to remain here for some time, and we feel like settling down and making ourselves comfortable.

We are divided into two parts as far as living is concerned. HQ's Flight and A Flight together, in a top-hole chateau, quite a new one. The owner lives in it himself, but they have one large room and bedrooms. As far as I can make out the owner is a first class spy for both sides, and the French would have shot him some time ago, only he gets them such valuable information. Rather amusing, isn't it? However, he seems quite a decent old boy though rather stingy. He owns a large factory near our aerodrome, and we others, B & C Flights, are billeted in workers' cottages. We have got a nice room in one of them where we all feed, and another for an ante room, so we are very well off. We are all more or less like brothers out here, and we try to eliminate hot air as much as possible. I suppose you would call it red tape. No doing stupid things for the sake of doing them when no good results.

Our work is now getting more lively. This patrol work is taken pretty seriously, and each one is given a definite sector to patrol, and hell is raised if you let a Hun through on your sector. We have our sort of trench warfare in the air. The archies are very hot out here. They are fearfully clever too, and a jolly lively time you get too if they are serious. If you get well into them they have a scheme by which it is impossible to turn away without running into them. We call it 'scissors'. It takes several batteries to work it.

The first of our fellows to go out on patrol thought he would like to see what archie felt like, and they fell so thick about him that he could smell them. He was above 10,000 feet too. However, they have got to hit vitally before they get you down, which is not very often. The Huns regard this as their defence, rather than by aeroplanes. At present, however, there is really no need for us to get archied, except that it must rather buck up the infantry.

I set off for my first patrol the other morning at 6.45 am (I am really getting quite good at getting up between 2 am and 3 am). There were a lot of clouds in the sky, but I found my way to the Lines all right. They are a weird sight from 10,000 feet, about which I was flying most of the time. I was patrolling a part of the line where the last big scrap took place, and in one part every inch of ground was churned up. In parts it is difficult to distinguish between English and Hun trenches. The whole line is dotted with redoubts and second and third lines could be recognised behind, sometimes with difficulty. It was really just a network of trenches, more in some parts than others.

In some parts there were towns and villages in the midst of this maze, and sometimes the line would run right through a village, and you could see trenches on the village green. It was a funny sight to think that all this mess is going on down there. Yet it appears to one, after a casual glance from above, that you only need go about two miles and you are through the whole thing. What impressed me more than anything else was that I was beastly cold after the first hour.

Occasionally I would come across another of our machines, and we would nose each other, to find out which side we were for. However, I know most English types. All round I could see archies bursting in the sky, not at me, but it was my business to see whether the product they were archying was ours or not. Towards the end of the first hour these bursts practically disappeared; I think the Huns must have been having breakfast. I did not observe any artillery work at that hour. The whole time I was well above the clouds, and as they became thicker it was less often that I could see the ground. It was an enormous field of billowy whiteness, stretching for days! Up and down I went mostly steering by the sun, when the ground was not visible for any length of time, always looking round and into Hunland.

At 8.15 I saw a machine in the distance coming at me parallel to the trenches on our side. I made straight for it and happened to be the same height. I edged off to get between it and the trenches so as to see whether he was friend or foe. It turned out to be a fast two-seater scout, painted pale blue-green underneath and looked thoroughly horrid. The observer was sitting up behind looking backwards with his gun ready to fire in any direction.

Of course he was a Hun so I simply banked into him to take him sideways, and fired a few rounds at about 300 yards, rather too far. Round he went to the left and away I went after him, again letting him have a few bullets, both of us doing vertical banks. I lost him for a few moments, and then saw him shooting for the Lines nose down. Off I went after him, but he had gained considerably, so I gave it up after getting across the other side of the Hun trenches. I was about 6000 or 7000 then, and had to get back.

As the greatest luck would have it, the archie fellows must have been still having breakfast, because I only heard about two 'poops' up at me. I can tell you I felt quite pleased with myself. I was the only one in the squadron to meet a Hun, and I had sent him on to his right side.

However, the whole thing had presumably been seen by an FE who reported that I fired at much too long a range, and a lot of other nonsense, so my CO wasn't at all pleased when I returned, and told me I had lost a chance. He is such a fearful fighter himself, and a wonderful pilot. However, better luck next time, it was only my tactics which were wrong. It is a most extraordinary game. Better than football yet something of the same. It is the same feeling to charge a Hun who sees you as it is to collar one of the biggest chaps in the school scrum.

32 Squadron, RFC, BEF, France, 18 June 1916
For quite a time we have been having just a sort of picnic out here. The weather has been dud day after day, the clouds always being so low. Nothing else would prevent our going up. However, it has been a most interesting time, I have been standing by from between eight to twelve hours a day, to go up at a moment's notice. If we were wanted up, we should have gone wet or fine. You will be interested to hear we have now got the Daylight Saving scheme out here now. It doesn't make any difference to us, as our hours have always been sunrise to sunset, and sometimes during the night too. I was on duty

last night, and consequently didn't get much sleep; I can tell you this is going to be a dud letter!

One little thing in Father's letter amused me awfully, as it never struck me quite like that before. It was about us all being 'heroes' to the French people, and saying we should be careful not to get spoilt by them. Now you need only be out here a few days to find out what small risks you run of being spoilt by the French people. You must remember that we are a part of that enormous body of the army who repose well behind the Lines, and that by the time No.32 came out here, the British had been in possession of this portion of the line for over 12 months.

We are often in the region of the HQ's of the big generals, and in any such place the streets simply teem with British soldiers. For the majority they certainly are not the sloppy lot you see in some of the English streets, but that is largely because there is some sort of order kept out here. Soldiers are not allowed to get drunk for one thing. I can tell you the people never trouble to look at you twice, they pass with complete indifference. The Flying Corps get a thousand times less notice taken of them out here than they do in England, except perhaps they are respected more by the rest of the army.

If the French people ever had any respect for the English soldier I should think it has mostly gone some time before I came. And I should imagine the blame for this could safely be deposited with the troops who 'fight' ten miles behind the lines. And if you only saw the French people I don't think that remark would have come into your letter. A more dirty crowd of people it is absolutely impossible to imagine. I speak mostly of the women, as there are no men, but I have no doubt they are equally bad. And the children wash only when they grow out of their clothes and *have* to take them off.

From what I had heard of France, I certainly received a shock. Possibly all the respectable people have departed and left the rubbish behind. However, this 'rubbish' has got some pluck. There is a large town near here, four miles behind the firing lines within easy shelling distance of the Germans. In fact it is shelled sometimes, only not too often, as we give it them back on another town. If you go into that town everything is normal, the shops are all open, and the people go about as if they had never heard of the war!

I am afraid the squadron has had a bit of bad luck lately. Poor old Stubbs has 'gone west' after his first patrol. He was seen being archied very badly, and later he was making for an aerodrome far

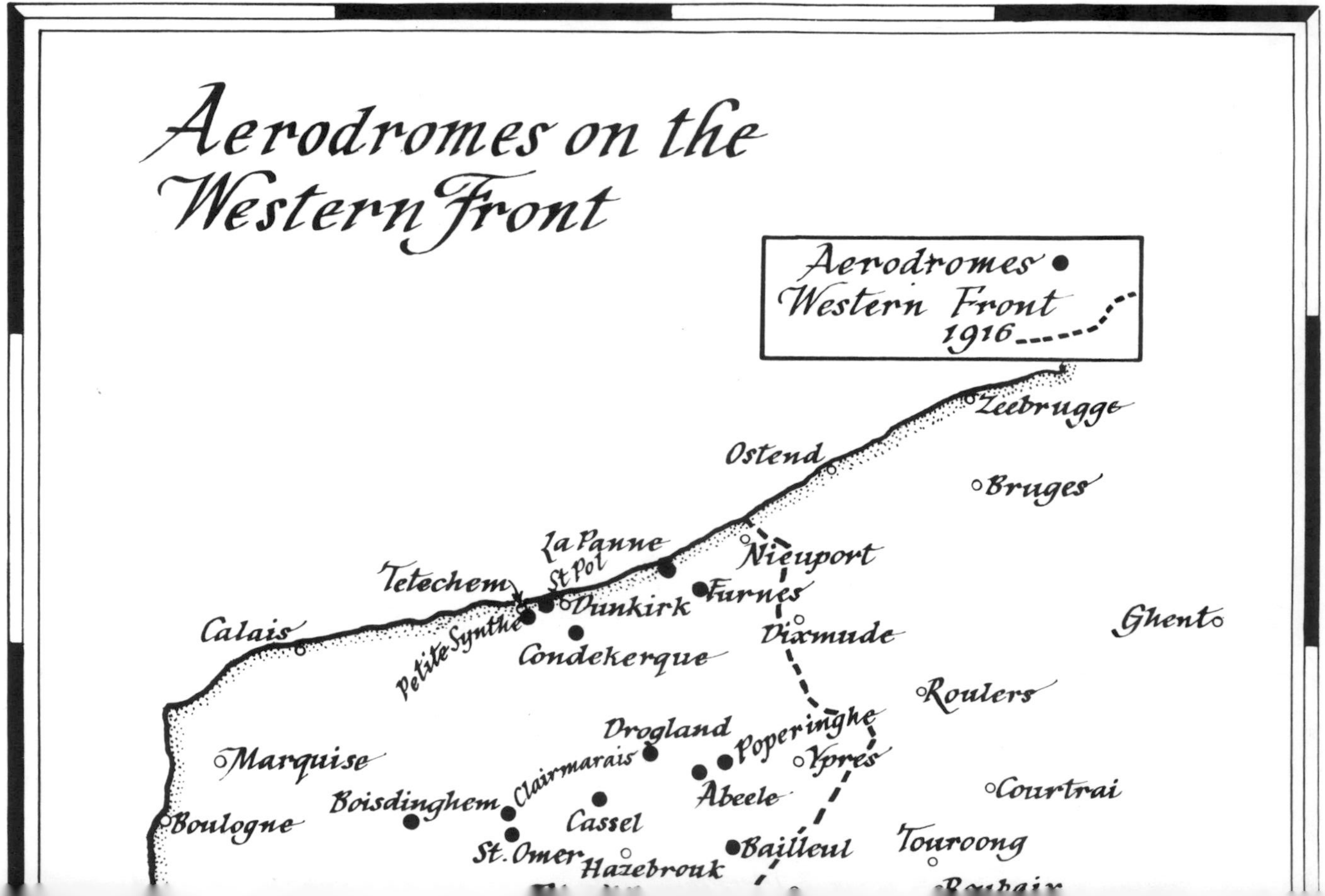

Aerodromes on the Western Front

Aerodromes·
Western Front
1916

Ghent

Bruges

Zeebrugge

Courtrai

Roulers

Ostend

Nieuport
Dixmude

Poperinghe

Yores

Furnes

Tourcoing

la Panne
St Pol
Dunkirk

Droglandt

Abeele

Bailleul

Hazebrouck

Teteghem
Petite Synthe

Coudekerque

Clairmarais

Cassel

St Omer

Calais

Boisdinghem

Marquise

Boulogne

Valenciennes

Henin-Lietard
Lens
Donai
Vitry
Marquion
Cambrai

Bryas
Houdain
St. Pol
Savy Aubigny Vimy
Le Hameau
Avesnes- Arras
le-Comte

Bellevue
Beauquene Lagnicourt
Fienvillers Leałvillers Moislains
Candas Vert Galand Farm
Warloy Senlis Albert
Bertangles Baizieux
Allonville
Amiens Chipilly
Cachy Cerisy
Villers-Bretonneux

N

0   5   10   15   20   25
Miles

0   25 Kilometres

E. G. M

south of the line, and when about 100 feet from the ground his machine put her nose right up and crashed horribly. He was killed instantly. Two slight grazes might have been caused by archies but it was just as possible that he had lost his way and had fainted, owing to the great height which he had been flying, to which none of us are very used to yet.[6]

The other day Captain Hellyer was starting out for an emergency patrol on my machine, when his engine gave out. He stalled on a steep turn down-wind and fell like a stone. No one ever expected to see him alive again, as it was a most hopeless crash, but he is pulling round finely. A few ribs and a smashed ankle seem to be the worst of the 'do'. He was my Flight commander, and one of the very best too. He had stopped a bullet when he was out before in a BE2c squadron. He will not join us again I am afraid. Another fellow from No.25 FE's was appointed the same day and went to St Omer to learn to fly a DH2. I am afraid he is now in much the same position as Hellyer. I think No.25 must be very bored as he was one of their best men.

After such a long rest we knew we should be in 'for it' as soon as we got a fine day. Yesterday it came, and some people got the 'fun' all right. Twice during the morning there was a certain amount of Hun activity reported, and both times I went up but saw nothing, it taking me too long to get my height after the message was received. The second time I went up with Henty after 10 Huns which were roaming about. I can't say I liked the idea, though if we had both got on to them, someone would have had something to think about. Neither of us saw them, as they had cleared by the time we were up there.

However, O.V. Thomas was on patrol at the time and bumped into them, and had a running fight for about half-an-hour. He singled out a single one rather below the others, but didn't have the luck to get him down. The old Hun was firing for all he was worth – a two-seater with the observer behind.

In the afternoon S.P. Simpson had a much more serious fray. He came across five Aviatiks and came up in the middle of the bunch. They all started pooping off at him, and he used all his ammunition on them, but again had the bad luck not to get the lucky bullet in. There is a good deal of luck in who gets the bullet home first. I never saw a Hun the whole time I was up, and I was up a good many hours. The day before I saw one about 9,000 feet below me on the other side of the Lines, but there was nothing doing as far as I was concerned. It is not often a chance like that comes, but I was jolly sorry for old Thomas having to take on the lot by himself. I should have been scared to death. However, in both scraps we had the speed of the Huns, but all the same you have to pull yourself together to charge a bunch like that. I don't know if I told you but the machine I met ages ago was a Roland, the Huns' best machine now, puts the Fokker in the shade.

Well, I must finish now. I was awfully amused to see you sent my letters about as if they were state secrets. I can assure you that I never put anything in a letter that would be of any use to the enemy, though a few things might interest him. I have not been out here three weeks without knowing a good deal though. Our Sector is so large that we always know when anything big is going on, and we also get army intelligence. I could tell you every Hun division on this front, and also that the vast majority of the Hun divisions have had a turn at fighting at Verdun. I also have reason for believing that the food question in Germany is ever so much more serious than we ever thought it was at home. Their army comes before everything, but even their army rations are much inferior to what they were. The feeding of *our* army is perfectly marvellous.

32 Squadron, RFC, BEF, France. June 25 1916
I am feeling rather fit for the moment, so I think I must write a letter. I couldn't tell you why I am feeling fit as yesterday I never felt cheaper in my life. I think it must be a combination of the fact that I had a bath yesterday and that I have been to Church this morning. You will be pleased to hear it is the third bath I have had since I have been in France, and it cost me at least 1/3d. Some enterprising French folk have rigged up three or four baths over a dirty little shop in the town, and very useful they are too!

Still more delighted will you be to hear that I partook in the service this morning, my second effort in that line since I have been out here. I think really it was quite a clever combination of cleanliness and Holiness! We have our services in one of our marquee, and a fellow from the town takes it. I attend when I can, but sometimes I am on duty. We had a harmonium too, you know, the squeaky sort, and our Intelligence officer played it; it was awfully comic when he was starting off on a new hymn, and working fearfully hard with notes and pedals, and the whole thing collapsed on his feet. I know it was bad for the discipline of the men, but I couldn't help laughing. However, they rigged it together again, and it went all right. The Padre is a jolly good fellow really, rather young, but he and I get on very well together. I suppose *I* am not so old either (Six Huns have crossed the Lines; our machines are crashing into the air. They won't let me go and I am itching to get up).

Our work goes on much the same as ever; we crash into the air at any moment of the day, and on any sort of day except a wet day. When in the air one gets beastly cold sometimes but not bored. There are usually half-a-dozen moments on patrol when your heart jumps into your mouth, and you swing your machine round and make for some blessed black specks. It is all very exciting. I cannot imagine what would happen if the Huns put up patrols too, right up and down the Lines. There would be a nasty mess, as we simply cannot bear seeing a Hun floating aimlessly about without asking him his business. We should go for him every time, much as we might long for an excuse to run away.

However, they have shown more activity during the last week or two than they have since the beginning of the war. They have actually carried out about half-a-dozen reconnaissances on our front since I have been out here. Never have they had less than five machines, and have even had eight, ten and twleve all at a go. Owing to their being able to fly so high, between 11,000 and 13,000 feet, they usually go back all right, but they appear to have terrible wind-up and I doubt whether their efforts were of much avail.

Nixon has done best for us so far. He is the fair, rather fine looking fellow who was speaking to Father at Netheravon. He is inclined to be nasal in his speech, and is the most fearless and brainless fellow I have ever met. He sighted five Aviatiks and closed right up on the rear one, at the same time emptying a drum. He changed his drum, attacked another, and got a bullet through his elbow. He tried to change again, but his arm was too stiff to do so, and there he had the agony of seeing the Hun trying to un-jam his gun. He had him sitting. He came down and made a perfect landing with his left hand. He had wires shot away, holes through his spar, and planes and rudder and tail plane, and everywhere he could want it. The machine had to be scrapped! I had left the Lines only ten minutes before they came across. I can tell you I was never so fed up in my life. Two DH's are fine company if worked properly.[7]

Three of our machines got into touch with 12 Huns the other day but didn't do much except talk when they returned. I think they

'Drachen Marsch' — a German observation kite balloon — usually nicknamed 'sausages' by Allied air crews — being man-handled to its operational base. Usually fiercely protected by a ring of ground AA and machine guns, an enemy balloon was no easy meat to attack.

dispersed the reconnaissance all right. When these Huns cross the Lines like this there is terrible excitement in the Flying Corps world. We always try to give them as good a reception as possible! I think they do the same for us, yet they have different methods. Unless these large bodies of Huns raid our side of the Lines, we never see a Hun at all. Perhaps occasionally a Fokker will be seen about five miles behind their side, but the usual thing is for him to turn every time we wink at him.

On the other hand it is perfectly astounding the number of our machines which cross their lines. Whilst on patrol one gets the full advantage of watching these beggars and return. You can see the archies bursting right away from the 'land beyond' long before you catch sight of the machines. And far away down below you can see the 'Lice', or BE's, doing their artillery work, and hopping back and forwards across the Lines, always to the accompaniment of the

32 Squadron's DH2 Scouts at Vert Galand farm, July 1916. On the right is the unit's second commander, Major T A E Cairnes between two pilots ready for a patrol. The farm in the background still exists, though the large barn has been demolished. One of the more famous RFC aerodromes during 1914-18, Vert Galand lay athwart the main Amiens-Doullens road.

An aerial view of Vert Galand aerodrome, taken in 1918, showing the improvements and additions made in the interim years. At the period during which this view was taken the aerodrome was in use by Nos.15 and 59 Squadrons RAF.

archies. *They* don't seem to care much!

The Huns do most of their ranging by 'sausages'. It is a great pity we haven't produced a first class two-seater biplane. I think engines is our great difficulty, as our construction, given scope, is far and away above the Huns. I should imagine we have to *pay* for our great increase in aerial activity, but the Huns do not get off scot free. I feel very confident that they have no love for crossing our lines, though our archies don't seem to worry them much. Yet Heaven knows what *we* would do without the archies. We can see their bursts for miles, and wherever there are bursts, off we go.

I will give you an idea how, while on patrol, years are continually taken off my life. The other day I was to go up with another DH and patrol the line with three FE's. I came in sight of the Lines at about 6,000 feet and there was our archie bursting all over the place down south. The other DH was about 3,000 feet higher and made for the bursts. I went off to pick up the FE's and dashed down the Lines. Any number of machines were there, and after a long fumble round watching the bursts, we saw five monoplanes at about 11,000.

I climbed for all I was worth and they gave us a dickens of a chase. At last we got fairly close and one of these beggars started to dive at one of my FE's. Down I went after him, and for the first time I saw he was plastered with 'rings'. You have no idea how relieved I was. However, the FE did not recognise him, and shot him down. I think he only hit the machine. These brutes turned out to be Moranes and had no business on our front. They were playing the fool too much. Later on they were being archied again, so I dived into the nearest one to make certain. He seemed quite all right so I threw him a kiss!

Before I forget I must thank Mother for a very excellent parcel of good things. They were all extremely useful and the cake, of which I was lucky enough to get one piece, went very well. The soap was rather 'suggestive', but in France you know we use nothing less than Pears!

P.S. I expect Edmund to be out here any time now. Martin from the CFS has joined us.

32 Squadron, RFC, BEF, France. 2 July 1916

Life is becoming what people at home would call very interesting out here. Interesting is hardly the word I should use, but I will not tell you what my word is, as it would look bad on paper. However, I admit that the daily paper is beginning to be worth its half-penny again, though if that noise I heard going on last night is 'war', I don't like war! Things have been just a little too lively for several of us during the last few days. We started off by strafing Hun sausages, which is very nasty. They repose about five miles behind the Line and direct their artillery fire. They hang up about four to five thousand feet, and it is a case of being archied the whole time. BE's, FE's and DH's took part in the show and dropped things on the brutes. It was rather cloudy and people lost themselves a bit, but out of our four there was only one to be seen on our front later on. These sausages are armed up to the teeth with guns.

The FE's next door are a most gallant bunch. They have been bombing and making reconnaissances the whole day long. Sometimes we have to join and sometimes not. We are always on the look-out to give a helping hand. They have suffered badly too for their trouble. We had a great stunt the other day bombing the biggest town on this front. About 25 machines must have taken part, and fairly threw their bombs about. I hope it isn't true that we are going to bomb the whole world. An awful nuisance if we do! There was a most awful gale blowing at the time. I should think about 50 mph up top. The machines simply crawled back across the Lines, archied like fury the whole time. Not a Hun was seen where there are usually plenty, so I suppose it must have been too windy for them. They are a 'windy' lot of brutes altogether. There have been numerous other efforts both night and day. Last night it was a sight to see the archies bursting in the sky. I suppose some day we shall consider the night the only safe time in which to fly. It's jolly unsafe during the day now!

The next day after our big raid, there being less wind, the Huns came over in one of their little bunches of eleven. J.C. Simpson, of Canada, met them and attacked them. Three detached themselves to attack. According to all trench reports he sent one of them down 'looping', then got his head in the way of a few bullets, and arrived just our side of the Lines. He was one of our cleverest DH pilots.

The Major (Rees) happened to be up at the same time on a DH. I told you he was the bravest man in the world. He came across them a little later, and the archie's batteries say they have never seen anything so gallant or comic in their lives. The Huns were in a tight little bunch when he came along – after he had finished they were all scattered in twos and ones all over the sky, not knowing which way

Major Lionel W B Rees, VC MC, the original commander of 32 Squadron RFC on its formation, and who thoroughly earned the award of his Victoria Cross for his action on July 1st 1916 when he single-handed attacked a greatly superior (numerically) formation of enemy aircraft.

to go. He sent the first one down out of control; the second one probably had a bullet through his engine. He turned to attack the third, whose observer was sitting with his head back and his gun aiming vertically upwards fairly blazing off bullets. I suppose he must have forgotten to take his hand off the trigger before he 'pipped out'. Just as the Major was going to get this machine as a trophy another fellow came and shot him in the leg from below. He was still going on but he discovered he couldn't steer his machine, so he came home.

He landed in the usual manner – taxied in. They got the steps for him to get out of his machine. He got out and sat on the grass, and calmly told the fellows to bring him a tender to take him to hospital. I am afraid he has got a very bad wound, though he is lucky not to have had an artery in his leg shot, as I understand he would never have got back if he had.

Of course, everyone knows the Major is mad. I don't think he was ever more happy in his life than attacking those Huns. He said he would have brought them all down one after the other if he could have used his leg. He swears they were youngsters on their first bombing lesson!! I don't know how he does it![8]

S.G. Gilmour takes over the squadron for a few hours. He was in charge of A Flight before, but has been put up for his majority. He went to escort a bomb raid in the evening and landed nearby with his machine all shot about and a bullet through his ear. A rather cheery day for us on the whole. I proposed a gamble on who is going to have the bullets tomorrow. A nice couchy wound would suit me all right. This is a dandy little war, isn't it?

Edmund has arrived here. He came here yesterday in spite of the fact that they told him he would not come. You see, the Major applied for him.

32 Squadron, RFC 10 July 1916
I always know when Sunday comes round owing to the fact that I do twice as much work, and I always do something that makes me remember it as a special day. The most interesting of these little occurrences was three Sundays ago – there is a road running alongside the 'drome, and if the weather is good, large crowds of French people congregate there. I thought I would amuse myself, so when taking off I went straight for them, and 'zoomed' right up over their heads. I certainly was very amused when I saw them pushing

'Going Over' – an FE2b two-seat 'pusher' on its way to the lines. A view frequently seen by its fighter escort during 1916-17.

each other about, and trampling on one another, but unfortunately my engine went 'fut' on the top of the 'zoom' through choking, a thing which has spelt death for so many pilots. I simply stuffed my nose down, and did a half-turn hoping to hit some sort of ground, dived under some telegraph wires, and by the grace of God I cut the petrol off and the engine gave a splutter, so I sailed up again and jumped another set of live wires, and went on patrol.

I found later that one-sixteenth of an inch on the fine adjustment made all the difference in the world. I thoroughly frightened everyone looking on, and the poor old Major was fearfully wild when I came down and said something about machines were expensive, and that if I wanted to kill myself I could stand in front of the butts at any time.

As regards flying, this week as a whole has been rather dud, yet the FE's have got through quite a lot of useful work. When I speak of the FE's I always mean No.25 as they are the other half of our Wing. I don't think I should be far wrong if I said they were the finest squadron out here. We in 32 have certainly learned to respect them. They do absolutely anything. During the last week they have been principally concerned with bombing, and as the days have mostly been dud, they usually perform at night. They have suffered rather severely lately, so we escort them regularly now. About one of ours to six when bombing, and three when on reconnaissance. I think I told you it was one of their fellows who shot Immelmann down. They say he was perfectly wonderful – the way he handled his Fokker, first stalling his machine, then diving absolutely vertically. It takes an awful lot of doing.[9]

Yesterday in the early morning there was rather an important reconnaissance on. Two FE's did it, escorted by four others and three DH's. Four Fokkers followed it round, but I don't think they cared much about attacking, as our fellows could be just as quick as they could. They usually like creeping up behind FE's on the way home. I expect they had Immelmann in their mind too, but how on earth they have got the courage to return to their aerodrome without attacking on *their* side of the Lines, I do not know. From all accounts one of them was a very fine pilot too, giving some wonderful demonstrations in the far distance.

In the evening I was on a bombing show. Six FE's were bombing a little spot and I was to be their audience. Through no fault of my own I was late in starting, so I made straight for the Lines, instead of rendezvousing as I should have. I crossed the Lines at about 9,000 feet and made straight for the spot which was to be smitten. There was a layer of clouds between eight and nine thousand. Just as I got over the place I saw the leading FE's signal for return; as I could only see four FE's returning I patrolled over there for about half-an-hour, just above the clouds, so that archie could only see me occasionally.

Later I saw a machine right away to the north, and thinking it was an FE hanging about I went over to try to hurry him up. As is usual in such cases he turned towards me, and I let him pass, and hanged if just as I let him pass he wasn't plastered with black crosses. I was just a comfortable 400 or 500 feet above him, and if only I could have known earlier I could have dived on him from the front, a possibility I have been dreaming of for weeks; I don't fancy these Huns' back mountings! Of course I swung round as soon as I could, and down went the fellow's nose into the cloud. I gave him half a drum as he was disappearing, when my gun jammed. I turned away to get it right again, which I did quickly as it was an easy jam, but I could not see him again. I expect it was an Albatros. I took very careful aim, but I don't suppose I hit anything as the range was rather long.

I am afraid it was a very dud show on my part, but you have no idea how frightened I am when I go for these brutes. I suppose he wanted to lead me over some archies, as I was just over a hot bed of them at about 7,000. I climbed another 1,000 and went home again. Archie was very dud that day, and I thanked Heaven for it, though I would not mind if he would send me comfortably home to get a little gold braid on my arm! By the way it is time I got my second pip. I have been in for it for about three weeks now. Do you know I have been out here six weeks now. It is six weeks too long for me in spite of the fact that I wouldn't go home if I were asked to. I can see it won't be long before I change my mind about that though!

We have got a new CO now. T.A.E. Cairnes is his name and he comes from No.27 – Basden's old squadron[10] I believe H.A. Taylor, a friend of mine in that squadron, has shot down a Roland, rather a stunt for a Martinsyde Elephant. They are down south now in the push. Do you know nine of the original pilots of No.32 are no longer with us; we are not half the squadron we used to be.

You know all about Edmund being here now. Of course he has quite settled down, and seems rather to enjoy the life. It's not such a bad little war if it wasn't so cold. Ed had two efforts to get in here first time, but that is absolutely natural for someone who has just come from the CFS aerodrome. After all this is only a very small-sized field. He seems to get in every time now all right.

From all accounts he has one nasty habit to be cured of. When he is patrolling with someone else he dives on them and practises 'S' turns behind their tails. He says he is preparing for Germans! I am afraid he will get shot one of these days. I know I would shoot him straightaway if he started doing 'S' turns behind my tail. Wait till he gets in a back-wash and suddenly his machine goes upside down, and he thinks he has got to drop 12,000 feet; he won't do it again! What do you think?

32 Squadron, RFC. 16 July 1916

Down south the 'show' has been going exceedingly well, I believe. Just lately we have got hold of some most excellent 'officials' and rumours. Incidentally not quite the same 'officials' and rumours as you receive in the daily papers, so I will, of course, not repeat them. However, I think the correspondents are given a very good time on the whole, now, which seems very wise.

I gather that we have only to advance a very few more hundred yards and we shall be fighting in open country. This line was no doubt chosen to attack on for very good reasons. Though very well fortified it was nothing like as well fortified as the line I patrol every day. The difference is most noticeable, and I think it is a great compliment to us that the Huns never expected us to attack across that line. It was only taken over from the French during the latter part of the Verdun show.

The Flying Corps has done jolly well down there, and by jove they have had their losses too. I cannot tell you how many. They have now gained a very reasonable superiority over the Huns, who are getting few and far between when it comes to fighting. Basden's old squadron (27) is down there and doing very well. Cairnes, our new CO, comes from that squadron. Taylor, a friend of ours, shot down a Roland, and has since been amusing himself bombing trains from about 300 feet. He blew off the front two coaches of one, and nearly got tipped up by the explosion. Sidney Dalrymple, who was with me at Hendon, also brought down a Roland at the same time as Taylor.[11]

I was speaking to a fellow who was in the first attack the other day. He has been out for 17 months now, right from the start! He says the

The author with his close friend in 32 squadron, Lt O V Thomas, 1916.

artillery preparation was wonderful, and he explained the whole process. He says his men went forward in the best of style and in perfect formation. His show was a failure. They got into the Hun first-line trenches which were something like a ploughed field, and found them full of Huns, Wurtembergers, everyone of which fought to the end, the end usually being a bomb or three bayonets through them. His battalion now has three officers, one sergeant, one corporal, and about 150 men. It is very probably up to strength again from England by now. He told me of one division which literally ceases to exist. Although he is very optimistic, as I think he has need to be, considering that the wretched Huns have got hardly any reserves, and will have to 'milk' their lines if they are to get men, and Douglas (*Haig*) is up to that!

We have started a few days' amusement in the shape of offensive patrols. This is a patrol about five miles over the other side of the Lines to make sure the Huns don't get inquisitive. Corby and I were

'Be it ever so humble ...' – the author at the entrance to his 'home', 32 Squadron, 1916.

to have the first kick-off, for two hours in the early morning, together with two FE's. I got up at 2.15 am, pushed a couple of boiled eggs down me and waited for daylight. We left the ground before 4 am being unable to see our instruments and it was beastly misty. The FE's being night birds got 'up' before us, and just as I approached the Lines I saw them cross, at least, I saw the archies. I have never seen such a show in my life, suddenly hundreds of shells seemed to burst into the air, and being half dark I could see the flashes. I actually thought 'at last I have found out why aviators are credited with having pluck', and for a few moments I thought I should never pull myself together to cross those Lines.

However, I caught sight of Corby's black outline, and he gave me the tip by crossing further south. We got across comparatively free, but as soon as we turned north those brutes started 'pooping' all round me. You can see them and hear them and smell them; three different sorts. It makes me laugh as I sit here now, but I really thought once that my nerve had gone, and that I should have to give up aviation. I know now that I was new to it, and that one gets used to this sort of show. As they never got any of us down their fire became less after a time, as they must have expended *many* hundred shells in those two hours. And it was the FE's which were drawing their fire most of the time too.

When you get about ten bursts up at you at once, it seemed silly to me to dodge about all over the place; I simply changed direction, and perhaps altered my height. After all they only hit me twice, once in the top plane, which was easily repaired, and once on the bottom plane. This necessitated a new plane, as it went through my main spar. Only three Fokkers came along, and all went home more or less the same way. They were trying to get the sun between themselves and us, and failed each time. I think I just happened to be nearest each time.

The first one I went for as he came down for me, at about 11,000 feet. As I approached reasonably close down went his nose in a most wonderful dive. I went down to 6,000 after him, followed by Corby, and could not catch him, he had too much lead. He must have been about 4,000 then. I climbed up again to 11,500 feet and again repeated the process to about 8,000, the other fellow still diving beautifully.

No sooner had I got up again than another brute came along and dived in the same manner. I followed him down to 4,000 feet, fired a burst, but could not catch him. I flattened out then and got frightened to death for a few moments as my engine would not pick up However, all went well and I found a nice tract of country where I wasn't archied. When I got to the end, archie went off, so I turned round and went up and down and returned home.

These little shows must have had a great moral effect on the troops of both sides, and I think the Hun archies got so fed up with their Flying Corps that they got quite dud towards the end, and showed very little life for the rest of the day. I think we four succeeded in 'fetching the price of our machines' out of the Huns that morning.

But that is not the end. About two hours after I had returned our archies reported a Fokker crashing west of a certain town, at a certain time. I think they said another one came down out of control. As I was the only DH doing anything at that time and at that particular spot, I have been blamed for it, though I have assured the colonel and everyone that I was totally unaware that I had been so cruel. On the next patrol Godlee shot down a single-seater biplane scout, just on their side of the Lines; it was shelled by us later, and Coleman claims to have shot a Fokker and seen it crash in a wood.

Our general is fearfully bucked with us. Out of seven Huns shot down that day by the RFC, three belonged to No.32, and we are therefore the first three who are allowed to put 'wings' on our machines – a little fad of No.32. Today it has rained most of the time, though a few fellows have been patrolling at 1,000 feet, well this side of the Lines. Edmund came very near to giving battle with a Roland this side of the Lines, but the fellow seems to have slipped away.

32 Squadron, RFC. 23 July 1916
Two months are up! It is just eight weeks since we departed in a merry bunch from Netheravon to try our luck out in this land of the dead. And on the whole I don't think we have done so badly. We have got a great name at St Omer, where they think we are better than either of our sister squadrons who have been out here longer. Of this I am doubtful, as one of these squadrons has done excellent work in the 'show' and, perhaps more than any other squadron, has kept the Huns more or less quiet down south. However, we have frightened any number of Huns, shot at plenty of others, with what effect we cannot tell, and we have shot down something like ten.

What is more important we have done something on the 1st Army front which has made such an impression on the Huns that scarcely

Opponent – a Fokker E.I scout on patrol, 1916. Pilot here is reputed to be Leutnant Kurt Wintgens (see note 20) but confirmation is doubtful.

Though of poor quality, a rare flying shot of a De Havilland 2 Scout on patrol. By the close of 1916 this design was well outclassed by its German fighter opponents.

Take-off. A De Havilland 2 Scout, piloted by Captain H W von Poellnitz of 32 Squadron, getting airborne from Vert Galand aerodrome in July 1916. Note the Flight commander's 'streamers' attached to the wing struts.

ever have they ever crossed our Lines after the first month, and not a single FE has been brought down while we have been escorting them, and only one attacked. The Fokker that did attack went down with one of his wings shot off. And during most of this period we have been taking the offensive and bombing every blessed spot that was worth a bomb.

On the other hand it is true that we are nine short of the original bunch of pilots. The ninth was Godlee, who, after escorting his FE's safely across the Lines, went back to attack some Fokkers who had followed the show at a safe distance. He is said to have sent one down spinning, when another one shot him in three places. He crashed well on our side of the Lines and died soon after. He shot down a Hun on the same day as I was supposed to have brought down a Fokker. What is more he was a pukka Anzac and a jolly good fellow.[12]

During the beginning of last week we were carrying out offensive patrols, three DH's and four FE's. Our usual course was over two Hun aerodromes, one of which we would drop bombs on alternatively, and then we would go to have a look at Lille aerodrome and come home. This used to happen three times a day. It was on one of these that Godlee got it in the neck. Edmund was on the same one but never saw the Fokkers. I only did one show, the weather being dud most of the time. We never got attacked the whole time, and archie was not offensive until I was returning near the Lines again, and then he started bursting just above me, which frightened me a good deal but never hit me. The reason for all this 'hot air' was because we have been having a little strafe of our own, principally as a diversion. It took the form of a big artillery demonstration on a limited front.

One afternoon I was patrolling where the strafe was at its height, at about 3,000 feet, just below the clouds. It was awfully interesting, but I was frightened of getting in the way of one of our shells. They were falling in hundreds all along the Hun front line with perfect regularity, some of them throwing tons of earth vertically upwards. The first one I saw I thought was a mine exploding. As I switched my engine off to come below the clouds, I could hear a fearful row going on. The Huns' reply was weak, and mostly gas shells I should think, as they gave off a horrid yellow-green smoke, most of which blew back towards their own trenches.

At 12.45 pm on Friday we were told we had got to move down south. By 1.30 we were all in our machines and following a leader to our destination. The leader lost his way, so after a heap of flying about the party broke up, and some got here and some didn't. I was one of those who didn't as I couldn't find my position on the map, having followed the leader blindly. I continued to follow him until he landed and crashed in a field. Three of us landed beside him, after he had given us the direction of the wind, one of which was Edmund. We found out where we were and flew here. The GOC, RFC met us and gave us a little speech. He said he had continually heard what good work we had been doing and told us why we had been brought down here. He said we must fight like the dickens during the next three days, and then the trick should be done. He said the C-in-C was always drawing his attention to the excellent work of the RFC. Prisoners were saying they got no rest in the rest billets or anywhere, and many of them wondered what on earth was the good of the Hun Flying Corps. They scarcely ever saw one of their own machines.

However, the fellows down here have had to fight like blazes since the show started, and as each new bunch comes along it has to be put down. The Huns wander around in bunches of eight Fokkers, or about 11 ordinary machines. All our patrols are across their side of the Lines, and we go in fours or sixes. If six of us get together we ought to do some damage! We had one little skirmish round the same day as we came here and some of the fellows had a tussle with a Roland, but he got away.

I went out with three others the next morning at dawn, but there was a ground mist, and we lost ourselves after a time, only having the sun to go by. This resulted in three of us again force-landing, and again Edmund was there! I don't know how none of us crashed, as it was a most precipitous and dangerous field. Since then the weather has been dud, so we haven't done our three days' strafe as yet.

The whole thing has been rather a come-down for me. I came to France to sleep between sheets and have a decent bed and comfortable chairs to sit on, and all those sort of things one couldn't get in England. I come here and have to put up in a tent, and sleep in a deck chair, and then get up at 3.30 am. What's more I had to shave in cold water! Although we are sitting something like 10 miles behind the Lines, the bombardments we hear are something terrific.

PS: I think our reply to the Huns' message about our 'Flying Corps' should be – 'For God's sake give your archies a rest!' The papers seem to have rather lost the humour of it.

32 Squadron RFC. 29 July 1916
Just a few lines before I buzz up on patrol to say that Edmund is quite all right, in case you have had some hair raising telegrams. He had a scrap with six two-seater Huns. He doesn't think he brought any down, but his machine got shot about all over the place. He has a slight flesh wound in his right ankle, and a few splinters in the pad and big toe of his left. He was able to hop about afterwards. I saw him this morning in hospital. He did very well and the whole squadron is very pleased with his performance.

32 Squadron, RFC, 30 July 1916
I have been up on a number of patrols. All our work is done well the other side of the Lines, and at times the place stinks of Huns. Yet they have their little dodges, most of which we are up to. So far I have not seen anything to attack, all the fellows I have seen have been very well their side of the Lines, flying harmlessly about at a few thousand feet from the ground. They know as well as I do that

32 Squadron pilots, July 1916. From left: Lts Bonnel; Inman; M J Maremontemboult; F H Coleman; Capt J.M. Robb; Lt L P Aizlewood; Capt H W G Jones; R H Wallace; Capt Nicholas; E Henty; G N Martin; Major T A E Cairnes (OC); Capt G Allen; Charles Bath; H W von Poellmitz; O V Thomas; G H Lewis (author), and P B G Hunt. Captain Robb eventually retired from the Royal Air Force as Air Chief Marshal Sir James Robb, GCB, KBE, DSO, DFC, AFC.

The LFG Roland C.II two-seater of 1916-17. Known to its crews as the 'Walfisch' (Whale), it was in fact an advanced design for its period, and gave excellent service.

archie is dying for us to come down! I am afraid I never feel quite comfortable flying about over there. We usually fly about in fours while the Huns are commonly found in eights or elevens. The worst of it is they very, very rarely attack us, and we always have to go for them,·which rather makes you pull yourself together and gives *them* a distinct advantage.

They have got their most daring (?) pilots opposite us now, and most of their machines are Rolands or a new type LVG which are very good. They have all got this blessed fellow with a gun sitting behind. Several of our patrols have had small rows with these fellows, but we haven't brought any down, and we haven't lost any. Before we came down here there were some terrible battles going on, and I dare say there will be some more later on. It is just about time I had another scrap. Not that I want one, as I get petrified with fear when I scrap, but I should love to bring a Hun down.

Edmund put up a very good scrap and everyone was pleased with him. I hear today that he has been moved down to base. He was very lucky to get back, as his machine was pretty badly hit about. We have got our rudder controls doubled, and when the machines arrive they have both these cables bound together. Most of us separate these two cables as soon as we get the machines and luckily Edmund had his separated. He had one shot away on each side, while if they were not separated they would both have probably given.

Four of us escorted 11 Martinsyde Elephants on a bombing stunt yesterday. It was quite fun, and the general was frightfully bucked in the evening, chiefly because no artillery machines were attacked.

I hear Miss R – is having the holidays with you. You can tell her that I still don't agree that the RFC is the softest job in the army. Apparently the infantry are the people who are most in awe of us. I was talking with some Anzacs and they seem to take the greatest interest in watching our machines, 'cheeky beggars' as they call them. A short time ago our fellows strafed the Hun balloons. This Anzac said all his fellows went mad with excitement, shouting at the top of their voices, shooting off their rifles, throwing their bombs about, and the artillery all joined in to celebrate the occasion!! One blessing about this front is that archie is not as a rule very active. Sometimes he is very good, but not very much of him unless he gets roused. He frightened me all right yesterday and made me jog about a bit.

Before I forget, I am no longer in the 10th Wing, so you can leave that off the letters. I wish we were back in it, it was a topping Wing, and I believe our old colonel rings up every day to ask when we're coming back. If you have any time, a couple of tins of Keatings Powder would be useful. I think it will help keep the bugs a little quieter!

32 Squadron, RFC. 6 August 1916
It is with a quiver that I write that horrid date on top. The eventful day has crept up to me and passed by, and left me with a horrid '19' beside my name. It absolutely scares me stiff to be getting old like this! I should always like to be 18; you can do just what you like and no one considers you responsible for your actions, so consequently one gets a jolly good time. However, I have to thank everyone very much for all the congratulations and presents I received. On the whole I think I did jolly well on my birthday both in letters and parcels. You see, Edmund seems to have left at the wrong time, because since he left parcels have poured into France for him. Of course, I open them without a moment's hesitation and take out

anything that looks good – so far everything has looked good. Mother's latest 'flea-bites' parcel should come in useful. It certainly contains all the latest devices for slaughtering bugs. Nesta's and Mary's peppermint creams have just come to hand, and are of the finest variety. We enjoy them muchly. Together with a large cake and two boxes of fudge which a fellow presented me with I have done pretty well. In spite of all my confounded old age I still maintain the responsible position of the youngest member of the squadron!

Things have been very lively during the last week. Many of us think we could well do with a short rest. Day after day is perfectly fine, and there is no change, or any signs of one. We shall patrol well over the other side of the Lines, and owing to a change in Wing, we are getting more work. Just lately the place has been alive with Huns, but they have shewn little desire to scrap unless the advantage is well on their side, and many are their tricks. Since we have been on this front only two Huns have come over, and our machines are always at work well over their Lines. I do not know what our mechanics would think if they saw hostile machines flying over their aerodromes all day. Our artillery machines swarm over the Lines, flying at anything from 1500 to 3,000 feet, and when they are ranging

Off duty. L-R; R H Wallace; J M Robb; L P Aizlewood; Corby and E Henty. 32 Squadron, July 1916, Vert Galand.

the big guns they have to go right across, mostly to the tune of archies, rifle, machine guns and small cannon. Sometimes one is attacked and perhaps shot down, but usually they go for their opponent and send him flying. It is too funny for words to imagine a BE2c driving off anything, poor defenceless old cows that they are. Some of the things RFC fellows have done in this show are too wonderful for words. One fellow used to fly at a couple of hundred feet up along the Bapaume-Albert road, strafing infantry and transport as he went along, and this on an old type Morane!

Basden's old squadron, 27, have done wonderfully well. I know nearly all of them as they were at the CFS with me. In particular H.A. Taylor, who has got the Military Cross. He dropped down behind Bapaume and bombed a train, and then shot at the engine driver. Seeing cavalry in a neighbouring field he zoomed at them, and forgot to fire his gun when he saw them scattering in every direction. I suppose he thought he was still on Salisbury Plain, where frightening soldiers was a favourite amusement. The same squadron made a bomb raid as far as the Rhine the other day, at least 300 miles, and after dropping his bombs on the objective Taylor again scattered infantry on the road, and someone else shot five cows!

During the last week our fellows have been scrapping every day. The Hun is usually pretty frightened of a DH and make a habit of putting their noses down when attacked. Each time we fire at a Hun we have to write out a 'combat report' and at the end of the last few days there has been a large pile lying on the CO's table. Personally I have done practically nothing. The other day I had rather good fun. A belt of clouds blew over the Lines lasting about five hours. We all lost ourselves and then tried to get home. We had a little reconnaissance which was rather important to do. One fellow got back here; the other three of us landed in various places. I landed in a topping French aerodrome, where there was a sort of reserve. They were very nice to me and gave me eatables etc. I found that I only missed seeing Joffre and Poincaré by about a couple of hours, as they had been making an inspection.

This morning Corby and I were escorting a BE who was taking photos. I was flying at between 7,000 and 8,000, and, by jove, archie took years off my life once with his high explosive shells. It is the nearest he has been for some time, and the row these things make is 'orrible! However, the Huns gave us a wide berth. In the last few days they have been getting a little more bumptious, though not much. Both their archies and their machines have had a little luck. Well, I have all the letters to censor, so must box up.

32 Squadron, RFC. 13 August 1916

For about 26 days now we have been doing offensive patrols without one day's rest, though about three or four days ago we jolly near had a day off, but not quite. We did Line patrols in a sort of semi-drizzle. Today there are a lot of low clouds floating about, and I haven't been up yet (4 pm) but I expect it will clear up soon. The last semi-dud day I managed to get off in the afternoon and took the opportunity of going to have a look at the scene of the strafe. We had to take some RE's up there and so Thomas, Hunt and I took the opportunity of going to have a look.

Monday – 14th

The blighters made me go up on patrol above the clouds so the date of my letter has changed. However, it was an uneventful patrol. I went miles out of my way to chase what I thought was a Hun on *our* side of the Lines. After a period of anything from three weeks to a month I caught up with him, and was just in the act of pushing my nose down at him to give him hell, when I perceived he was a Martinsyde Elephant! I left him in a hurry and then old archie started to throw his HE up at me with vim. When he had just about got my height and made me feel all of a dou-dah, I side-slipped a few hundred feet and ran for home.

Before I started talking nonsense I think I was telling you that I made a journey to have a look at the war. It was a most wonderful sight, and one I shall never forget. I must say I felt rather like an American sight-seer, at any rate I could imagine them doing exactly the same things after the war is over. Along one of the roads we went along, absolutely as straight as a die, there was a never-ending line of troops, for about eight miles, consisting of all arms all going one way. We went through the old British and German first lines, and part of the German second line, or I suppose it would be an auxiliary line. The whole place behind the German lines was a mass of shell holes, and their trenches were hopelessly knocked about. Their wire had been smashed to bits, and was practically useless.

I went into a little officers' dug-out, now in use by some of our officers, and had a drink. It was dug nice and deep into the ground and built up of huge wood beams, and with a roof of railway lines and plenty of chairs and tables. I did not notice any electric lighting or water supply, though I have no doubt plenty of them are fitted up with these delights. The Hun first line was also well stocked with these 40-foot dug-outs for the men, not a single one of them seemed to be seriously damaged. I went down one and it smelt most unholy. The floor was littered with Hun trousers and equipment. It wasn't at all decent. Most of the time we were playing about in what was once a village. There was nothing left of it at all, so far as I could see. I shouldn't have known it was there at all if I hadn't been told. The roads were kept up wonderfully considering they are always being shelled. Later on we had a look at a couple of mine craters, nearly large enough to take our house in, complete with furniture!

We were something like a mile behind the present first line. You see, we didn't believe in getting hurt! Besides there was a lot of strafing going on and we could hear the shells buzzing up into the air and coming down with a 'plonk' just to our right. They scared me at first, but after that I wanted one to burst right near me to see what it looked like. I don't suppose I should have asked for two! We soon came across a six-inch howitzer battery in action. Quite a fluke we found it, of course, because their shells don't make much noise. It was awfully interesting watching it, and we stayed there some time, always being ready to jump into a trench and hide ourselves if the Huns got wild about it. Standing behind one gun we could follow the shells right up into the air until it went into the clouds. The clouds were about 5,000 feet. Later on we saw one of our archie guns having a little fun. A Hun had wandered a little too close up to the Lines and gave me a shock. I never knew a Hun ever came so near as that. I have kept a better look-out since. I picked up a few time fuses and one or two things like that. Also a few of our 18-pounder shell cases, which I hope will get home some day. There were a few unexploded 15-inch shells about, but I thought I would leave them, as I have heard they are a bit dangerous when they go off.

Life in the air has been much the same as usual. Plenty of archies and plenty of crawling Huns. They are getting a wee bit braver now, though they never attack us, we always have to go for them. Most of our time is spent in diving after low Huns. They fly low so as to give their archies good sport when we come down for them. I dived on a few singles who I thought were getting too near their Lines and they stuck their tails between their legs and went scraping the chimney tops of the nearest town. I usually give them a drum to go home with, just to show there is no ill feeling! I had one more exciting scrap. I was leading a patrol of three machines on a terribly misty day. We could only see vertically down. The other two fellows were Aizlewood and Jones. We were flying at about 12,5000 feet when with the most appalling suddenness six Huns appeared 6,000 feet below. I don't suppose they were doing much harm, but I thought I had better let them know there was a war on. So down I went, followed by Aizlewood at anything up to 130 mph. Jones stayed up on top to protect our backsides. The Huns, probably Rolands, thought six to two was good enough so they waited. We each chose a Hun and gave him about a drum, their machine guns going crack-crack-crack all round. I had a gun stoppage so I swung round to get it right and change my drum. When I got fixed up the Huns had fled towards their own Lines. We three got together again and climbed up to 11,000, archie having his little bit of fun too. We sallied out again and with appalling suddenness again, five similar bounders appeared below. They were obviously the same lot, so I feel certain we sent one home for repairs the time before!

Aizlewood and I went again, but this time I fooled them. There were four together in a small bunch in front and one a wee bit further behind (these Huns kept jolly good formation). I dived for the front four, and just as they were getting all excited and ready to shoot me down with their four guns, I swung round and simply let fly at the last fellow, giving him a topping spray of bullets. However the other fellows were so wild with me that all five let fly at once and I could see and hear their bullets all round the place. Of course I knew the four fellows in front had little chance of good shooting. The last fellow soon had enough and stuck his nose down and went home. Aizlewood came down a bit low and made him stick it down still steeper. Jones was on top and he said the other four pushed their noses down for home too. All I know is that I found six little holes in my planes when I got back, causing one of them to be changed. If *they* cost me one new plane I'll swear I cost that back fellow two. The most amusing part of the story I learnt when I got home. When we dived the first time a Fokker appeared from nowhere and pushed his nose down after us. However, old Jones was too smart for him and gave him a few bullets which sent him on his last dive! Jones was out on his first patrol, and is such a bad pilot that he is being sent to a BE2c squadron! Rather an effort on his part I think.

Capt L P Aizlewood, MC seated in DH2, 7907, 32 Squadron. Of interest is the red/white/blue 'ring' marking on the wheel fabric cover.

The other day Sergeant Dobson separated himself from his patrol and was seen to be shot down by four Rolands who slunk up behind him. It is always dangerous to leave the patrol.[13] Captain Gilmour had a cylinder blown off his engine and crashed in a shell hole, breaking his nose. I have no sympathy with him because I was on patrol with him at the time. The sun was behind us and he simply went out and *sat* over archie. At one time I saw him go down for a Hun, and I couldn't get near as there was a sort of barrage of archies between myself and him, and everyone knows I get petrified with fear when archie coughs round me! I simply prayed that some would hit him and send him home!!

32 Squadron, RFC. Sunday, 10 September 1916
I am back on the old job again, and the old writing pad, which was, incidentally, sent out for Edmund's benefit. Before I went on leave I thought I should feel so pleased about having had a week's peace, that I should become quite a bold aviator. But instead of that I was all of a dou-dah and shivering in my boots; not a bit what a member

of a fighting squadron should be. However, a dive or two soon put me in my place and I feel quite fairly fit again. I enjoyed the leave most awfully, quite a change from this game out here. We had quite a peaceful trip back here. It was a bit bouncy on the crossing, which made Thomas feel a bit wonky. It was quite amusing trying to walk from one end of the boat to the other in a straight line. However, we felt very safe as his Lordship, the PM, was on board and our escort was accordingly numerous.

Apparently there had been a certain amount of activity while we were away. The Huns have got just about every squadron they ever possessed on this front, though things are not changed a great deal. It is necessary to keep a brighter eye open and prepare for action. Our artillery work still goes on, only better looked after, and *they* do just about as much as they did before. Scrapping is pretty well the order of the day, as Hun patrols are rarely composed of less than a dozen machines. However, four of ours managed to disperse a patrol of 13 the other day. I am afraid Bainbridge dived amongst 14 of them, and I fear went down out of control. He was a very recent addition from England, and had little flying experience.[14] Poor old Wilson, (Capt. R.E.) has also been knocked out, though he landed under control in Hunland. We miss him badly, as he was a cheery soul, though I fear too fond of whisky. However, a few months on black bread should do wonders.[15] Both Curphey and King have brought down two Huns, without doubt, out of control, while several other Huns have been certainly hit.

Since my return I have done nothing very exciting. The evening I returned we bumped into a large bunch of HA's (hostile aircraft). I was practically unserviceable from the start, as my engine had cut out on two cylinders and I was slowly losing height, and all the enemy were well above me. There were plenty of our machines about, and I satisfied myself with diving after a machine which was going down in a great hurry, and turned out to be a Nieuport. After that I crept home. I forget half the things that happen these days, but I remember Hunt got a very nasty time yesterday afternoon. He was escorting when two very dashing Rolands attacked him from above. They dived time after time, but at each effort he managed to turn sharply into them, so that they overshot him every time. He was unable to fire a shot. I feel very ashamed of myself as I was on patrol at the time, and certainly should have seen what was going on. I came along soon after, and these two brutes did a couple of circles

A cheerful group of 32 Squadron's DH2 pilots, 1916. From left: W G S Curphey; E Henty; F H Coleman; J J G Maremontemboult; Capt R E Wilson. Wilson later became a prisoner of war, the 20th victim credited to Hauptmann Oswald Boelcke, leader of the German Jagdstaffel 2.

above me before I discovered they were Huns.

At this point a good many of our machines came along so these fellows cleared off home.

Later on in the evening the patrol attacked several Huns. Captain Aizlewood was so engrossed in his Hun, and so cut up that his shots were having no apparent effect, that he rammed his opponent. His undercarriage swept along the Hun's top plane and engine and broke off, while one of his tail booms was cut by the Hun propeller. The Hun was witnessed by many to go down out of control and crash, while Aizlewood still had more or less control of his machine. It was swaying about terribly however, and the nerve strain of more or less waiting for it to fall to bits must have been terrific. He managed to land behind our Lines completing the wreck of his machine. He is perfectly all right, but his nerves are obviously affected, and he has got a fortnight's leave. Quite a good show, don't you think, considering he is quite a level-headed, yet very keen fighter?

32 Squadron, RFC. 17 September 1916

All sorts of exciting things have been happening during this last week, and I know I have been doing an 'orrible lot of work, but my memory only dates back to the 15th. Before that everything is a blank! We were very excited some days before. Rumours would keep coming through and we found all sorts of lively things in store. These walking tanks have been a tremendous stunt and kept very quiet; they are perfectly priceless animals; nothing can stop them, they simply walk on and on, over trenches or ditches or anything, and finish up by enfilading a trench. Put the wind up the pigites all right! It was very interesting hearing the plan of operations the night before; and then everything went finely on the 15th. We captured all our objectives and — which wasn't one.

We were all prepared for a tremendous amount of work but I didn't get much. I was looking out for Hun transport and all sorts of things to go down and have a pot at, but I think they run everything underground. It would have been splendid fun to have turned a waggon over in the road. All we did was scare a few Huns and make them scuttle for their lives. On another patrol a Hun got on one fellow's tail, and by all the laws of the air should have brought him down, but this fellow, Maremontemboult, was too smart for him, and sent him down 'roast pig', poor fellow. Most of the fighting was done far the other side. Thirteen Huns in one day is a pretty good bag, isn't it? And you can be sure that they are all certainties as near as it is possible to gauge. If they are not witnessed they would probably come under the heading of the nine badly damaged.

Yesterday I got a little shooting practice; it really was quite absurd. There was a thin layer of clouds at about 7,000 feet. Nicholas was leading the patrol, and I was alongside Thomas. I spotted about eight Huns below, so I attracted Nic's attention and down we went, fired a drum and went up again. The Huns simply pushed their noses down and showed their tails, as far as I could see. This went on for the rest of the patrol; everytime we got up Huns appeared round Bapaume. I think the patrol fired 13 drums off in all! We probably got some hits, but I think we were all a lot of funks. We wouldn't close on the fellows properly. Personally I hate having all their guns firing at the same time.

I went down to 4,000 one journey, and Thomas went down to 3,000 on another. And then old archie would start. He nearly blew me out of my seat once. I hunched my shoulders up and put my head down; I thought he was trying to blow my head off, the dirty dog. Old Corby went down to about 400 feet and fired into Hun trenches. I bet he fired into our own! I found I still had another drum left at the end, so I tried to put Transloy on fire. I understand it is still burning!

Today the HA's have been singularly inactive. It is rather amusing to see that old Boelcke is taking to flying again. I should like to shoot him down, though I suppose one isn't much good if you don't get a Zep down these days. Poor old Robinson must regret ever having performed at all. His life isn't worth living. All the risk that I can see he took was the coming down again, though of course as a feat it was magnificent.[16] I would rather attack one of those gas bags than a couple of fighting Huns any day, and as for attacking a Hun balloon – well –. You will be glad to hear Aizlewood has got his Military Cross, as we expected. He's a jolly stout fellow. Nixon has come out again, but unfortunately has gone to No.24. I am sorry to say that Bentley has killed himself today, by stalling on a low turn while landing. It was horrible.[17]

32 Squadron, RFC. 25 September 1916
It was rather amusing to see how the base-censor had tried to rag my letter the other day. I suppose he was some little flea-bite of a Second Lieutenant who once heard a couple of shots fired, so retired to the base in order to wear a blue tab on his collar. At any rate, his efforts were quite unnecessary as I only mentioned the names of towns that had appeared in the 'official', and I presume the Huns know that they have lost them, in spite of the fact that their archie doesn't. He seems to have a complete disregard for the present boundaries, which surely is very bad form!

Everytime I write I always forget to thank everybody for all the things I receive. I suppose I get so many things that I lose count. The box of 'whiffs' went round in great style, there being very few refusals. The books were excellent. I have already read two or three of them. *Septimus* was great; it kept me laughing all the time. I was awfully interested in those letters of Rosher's.[18] He must have been a jolly good fellow, and even in these days when half the fellows in the Corps earn a VC every other day, his stunts stand out as very remarkable. But what is most surprising is the total lack of 'hot air' in his letters. I mean nearly everyone puts in a bit of 'hot air' in their letters home, so as to be sure to get another cake.

And that reminds me that I have just got hold of a large parcel containing all sorts of exciting things like pyjamas and meat tablets, and all those things that make life worth living. Also as letters and parcels are most consistently sent here for Edmund, I send on his letters and keep his parcels! I got a jolly good cake that way! His address is No. 2 Aircraft Depot. He came here to dine a few nights ago, and the other night we dined together with Basden's old squadron. I think he is getting pretty fed up with life.

I have just been watching some Huns who have come right across our lines, nearly as far as our 'drome. Quite sporting of them to come. We love seeing them. A jolly fine chance for some dashing young aviator, if he can strike one on our side. However, it is rather misty.

The first part of this week was pretty dud, but the last few days we have had our money's worth. I think we have knocked down about six Huns. King started off one evening by catching a Hun doing artillery work up north. The fellow was very low and I suppose thought he was out of danger; nevertheless he crashed to the ground. King again repeated very nearly identically the same show next morning. Then I came along and sent a Roland scout down in a bit of a spin. Jones followed by knocking a Hun down, and saw it fall among some bursting shells. One burst on it and the machine was seen no more. Then Jones drove another one down and made it land; while Henty followed suit with another Hun.

As my effort happened on quite the most exciting patrol I have had I might tell you about it. As soon as I had got up to the Lines I got terrified stiff. I was well above the rest of the patrol when a Roland passed right over me. I couldn't see his crosses until he was right over, and then I could see the observer looking over the side with his gun pointing right down at me. However, he forgot to fire. I am sure I went as white as a ghost; you know how helpless we are if people get above! So do I!

I watched him with considerable interest for some time, when I suddenly caught sight of a BE12 fighting for his life with two Huns right down low about eight miles over the Hun Lines. I was some distance away but, of course, I dived down as soon as I could. I dived down to 4,000 when to my horror I saw three other Huns come down too. I quite thought I had got to fight for my life, and I don't remember ever being quite so frightened before.

However, I got close up behind a Roland and emptied a drum into him, and he went down in a spin. I put another drum on in a most desperate hurry and, of course, a bullet jammed as I was putting it on. I soon got over that and, looking round, I saw a fellow on my tail. So I did a most hurried turn on a wing-tip and gave him a drum. He soon got fed up and went down.

Since I had come down I had not even caught a glance of the BE. I changed another drum and again I found a fellow on my tail. I again jumped round, and hanged if he wasn't a BE12, and not a Hun in sight. So I felt awfully cheery to think that everything had gone well and that the Huns were scared off. We departed in triumph therefore and waved to each other, while the Hun shot up every imaginable invention of the devil from the ground, including a sort of Roman Candle which was supposed to put us on fire. It went right over my tail.

When I returned I found that the BE that followed me was another BE12 who had come down after me, which made me awfully sick. No one seems to know what happened to the other fellow. The next day a French Nieuport confirmed my belief that the Hun went down out of control. So much the better for me. Later on in the patrol I dived on two lots of Huns, getting off a drum each time, but it was so much wasted ammunition.

32 Squadron, RFC. 29 September 1916
A dud day, so I have had the opportunity of looking through a pile of correspondence, which ought to have been attended to a long time ago. Amongst other things I see your very kind offer to send me a 'Chemico Body Shield'. Now the only way I can express my sentiments is to say that even if I had the money I should certainly never buy the thing, yet I cannot help thinking that if I were to refuse your offer I should be a fool. There is no getting away from the fact that the thing *might* work, and as I have always more or less kept to the 'prevention is the best cure' touch, I should certainly not feel too proud to wear it. In fact I actually had a steel bottom put to my seat the other day when I thought I might go down low, if I thought there was a chance of doing good.

Another point to be remembered is that one's *eyes* are one's one and only friend out here, and it would be absolutely out of the question to put anything on which would prevent one being able to twist one's body and look about properly. People who have sharp eyes and know how to use them start off with an enormous advantage at this game. One must never go to sleep! To sum all this nonsense up, I accept your very kind offer, Dad, if you are convinced yourself the thing is good and practicable.

We are all awfully bucked to see in today's *Daily Mail* (Thursday) an interview with Boelcke in which he says he shot down our Captain Wilson, and that Wilson is perfectly undamaged. Wilson had been through the East African campaign and was a great spark in our Mess. He was always merry, but drank much too much. However, as I said before, black bread will probably be his cure!

I hope everyone is keeping happy and well. We have been worked half crazy lately, but our morale is at the *top* hole.

32 Squadron, RFC. 1 October 1916

We have been confoundedly active; in fact I think it has been a record week, in spite of the fact that we have had one completely dud day. The going-up part isn't half so boring as the continual waiting about ready to go up at a moment's notice. Well, there is certainly nothing to grumble about as this squadron has had most remarkable luck as regards losses. Soon after I wrote my last week's letter we got a special congratulation from our GOC Flying Corps for our work during the previous week, and in some respects we have kept the pot boiling. Everything has been usual except that the Huns are getting braver. I have gone in for the usual dashing about and fruitless expenditure of ammunition. In fact it is becoming quite uncommon to return with all your drums full. If I can't find anything better to fire at I empty a drum into villages or dumps, or Hun trenches; it bucks the infantry up. However, I never feel brave enough to go down low like Corby did. He went down to 400 feet over the trenches; about 20 Hun machine guns immediately came into play, so to show that two could play at that game he fired his gun amongst them. When I do it it's always from a respectable height.

I think Curphey set the ball rolling again this week. He is commonly known as the 'dirty little Scotchman', or 'Growler'. He was quite alone when he stealthily slipped over the side of a cloud onto a perfectly inoffensive Hun, and watched it disfigure a beautiful wood. The next day Aizlewood, who has returned from leave, dropped on a less inoffensive Hun, and sent him down in a spinning nose-dive. He managed to get out of this, however, so Curphey went for him, and put him in another spin, and watched him disappear through a low cloud. Someone else saw him on the ground later. We

Veterans. Capts W G S Curphey, MC (left) and L P Aizlewood, MC of 32 Squadron, 1916. Curphey was shot down in flames on May 14th 1917 and died of his injuries the following day.

have great hopes that Curphey will get a Military Cross.

Today being the Sabbath something exceptional was sure to happen. There was a patrol of five up knocking about Hunland. The last two of the patrol were scrapping for their lives against three Huns above them, while the front three went sailing gaily on not knowing anything about it. Martin, the patrol leader, actually had a bullet through his tail boom and was none the wiser. The Huns finally decided to leave our fellows alone. Later on Von P. and Bath of the same patrol went jogging along, when a Hun all but bumped into Bath, neither party knowing the other was there. Bath suddenly saw the fellow just below him and was unable to get at him, so Von P. had a shot, and sent the poor fellow down in flames. Von P. has previously sent a Hun down; we believe these are the only two Huns he has seen since he has been out here – he is as blind as a bat![19]

Another interesting part about this wonderful day, bar the fact that I have done two patrols, is the fact that King and Jones have both been shot down, and both are all right. Jones has landed amongst the most thickly populated shell-hole districts out here, and his machine is a complete wreck. King managed to get further across and has landed safely. We don't know the details yet. It is probably that brute Boelcke. I am keeping an eye open for him. We will get him yet. You notice we have got Wintgens.[20] Nixon, whose name you will remember, has come out here again, and joined a sister squadron, got shot down the other day but scrambled our side of the Lines. *He* doesn't care.

I am very troubled about Taylor of Basden's squadron. He and another fellow were shot down the other day, and one went down out of control and the other was all right. We don't know which is which. I was only dining with him about two nights ago too. They go such long miles over the Lines.[21]

32 Squadron, RFC. 8 October 1916

There is very little to write about this week except perhaps the rain and clouds. The west wind has been hard at work all the time, so that on the whole we have been forced to let him have his way and lie low. Perhaps the most interesting day of the whole week was when a party of us sallied out to see the war. We took a tender and drove up in style, our object being to see a tank if possible. We soon found one, as we had expected, but it was more or less blown up, yet fairly complete. We all got inside and examined things, picked up bits of old iron as souvenirs and generally made ourselves at home. Later we found another of these brutes and had a good look at that. It was of a different type but equally interesting. One is called the 'Male' and the other the 'Female'. As would be expected, the 'Female' looks the most dangerous, though I can't say either of them looks very friendly.

Well, we wandered on and on. There was a good deal of shelling going on, and a nasty horrid row; at least 20 aeroplanes were knocking about just over us, and old Hun archie was getting unpleasantly close to some of them. Hun shells were bursting all over the place, but not too close. You could see them kicking up dust in front, and others passed right over us. We finally got to a spot where we had a most delightful view, just by a mound. It was most interesting looking into Hunland at places that we know so well from above. Thomas and I were having an ardent discussion as to which place was which, when a little man in a tin hat came along from a battery and advised us to move, as about 50 Hun batteries were ranged on that mark, and it was probably the most dangerous place in France! When I get home I will tell you that we were standing alongside what was once Pozières windmill. Just at that very moment the Huns must have thought it was time we moved because they whizzed over a '59'. Down we all went like clockwork, and then the rout commenced. It must have amused the countryside somewhat to see the 'gallant RFC' in utter rout. We ran for all we were worth scrambling in and out of shell holes. Then a beastly shell would come over, and down we would throw ourselves flop on our faces in a hole while it burst, then up again, for all we were worth. It must have looked jolly comic and, frightened as I was, I couldn't help roaring with laughter each time I threw myself down in a shell-hole, and I can tell you I went down with some vim! I dare say it was all quite an unnecessary performance, and I don't suppose one burst within 50 yards of me, but Henty got splashed all over with mud. However, it was a very amusing afternoon, and we finished up the day with a very excellent dinner.

P.S: Curphey has got his MC, which is very satisfying. He is an awfully stout fellow.

32 Squadron, RFC. 15 October 1916
The wind has continued to howl from the west carrying a continual stream of very low clouds and rain. When flying has been possible it

hasn't been very comfortable for single-seater scouts, which turn over rather easily, as the wind has always been blowing in the form of a semi-gale; and then when one crosses the Lines with about 50 miles of wind about it becomes very anxious work getting back again, especially if archie is getting closer and closer and a Hun creeps up after you from above. The last time I was up the Huns took full advantage of the gale and came much nearer to their Lines than they are supposed to. I know I felt very uncomfortable with two HA well above me, and in spite of the fact that I climbed to about 13,500 they were still above, which is very demoralizing.

We shall have to bring out some very fine machines next year if we are to keep up with them. Their scouts are very much better than ours now on average, and by jove some of their pilots know how to fly them too, as Maremontemboult will tell you, as he got shot down the other day, but was unhurt. And also Hunt, who finally managed to creep off by doing a spinning nose dive, and on the way down shot the Hun off Maremontemboult's tail as he was endeavouring to creep to our side of the Lines. This is not the first time Hunt has shewn great judgment in combatting two very clever Hun scouts, both in superior positions and on better machines. It takes a bit of doing, and it is in such times that one's presence of mind is tested, and some of us find it lacking, alas!

I forgot to tell you that about three weeks ago we moved out of our tents owing to the bad weather, and shifted into a farm close by, where we are now billetted in the loft, and very comfortable we have made it too. We have swept all the cobwebs away, and built partitions, making quite nice little rooms. There are enough windows to go round, and I share a patch with Henty, who I also shared a room with up north. I don't know why we do share as we sometimes get quite annoyed with one another, and remain peevish for quite a long time. On the whole though we mug along quite happily.

For a considerable time our thoughts have been all centred on winter, and the change in conditions we were going to get, and consequently we have been preparing. For quite a long time we have been building a nice little Mess for B and C Flights, and two or three days ago we moved into it. We have knocked four Armstrong huts into two parts, one of which is the Mess room, and the other a very comfortable ante-room. The huts have got a nice wooden floor, and on top of that we have put some very swagger linoleum, and pretty mats in the ante-room. We have made a beautiful oval table for the Mess, which seats anything up to 18, and we have chairs to sit on, which are more select than the biscuit boxes we used to have. There is not the same temptation to push the next fellow off his box. In the ante-room we have another array, and very comfortable chairs, and to cap everything we have bought a stove for each room. Nearby we have put up a nice kitchen, and have bought a very swagger stove, on which we cook all sorts of things. I don't mind telling you that last night we had a couple of very excellent roast duck! Our cook, who is one of the servants, is becoming very proficient, in spite of the fact that he knew nothing when he came out here. Of course, sometimes we have peculiar looking dishes, but that is all in a day's work. That does not frighten us nearly as much as when the servants start singing in unison in the kitchen. When this happens there is a rush for the gramophone!

When we begin to feel a little bored we can always have a good hearty quarrel with the lady of the farm. She is really a very kind-hearted dame, but she has peculiar ideas about noises we make in her loft at night. She seems to object to any stampeding, or water thrown about, or any of these amusements which make life worth living. A few days ago we had a row which went on for a complete day, resulting in half the Interrupters (Interpreters ...) in France being present. But she is such a hearty talker that there is little to do but to listen. She started off early in the morning, and one of the fellows half-awake asked what the new gramophone record was!

However, on the whole things go very well and we try to be good. The other day though there was a bit of a fuss. We had nothing much to do so we captured one of her cocks, and after a good chase got another one from a neighbouring farm yard. Things were becoming interesting when the good lady came in, so we had to scatter the cocks in a hurry. The major, who had wandered up and was enjoying the show, had to scurry round one side of the building while she came round the other side and cut for it. You see it is most improper for COs to attend cockfights! There is another squadron in the neighbouring loft who are sometimes given to exhibiting a little too much life, much to the annoyance of the old fossil who owns the farm. He came stamping up to the loft and they invariably come forward to meet him with the words, 'Oh yes, we know you. You have come to fly our new scouts, haven't you?', and this usually pacifies him.

This morning I set out with V.P. on a 'defensive patrol'. I soon got tired of following him, however, so I wandered off on my own. After about an hour's flying I found a Hun, on whom I bestowed a drum, after which he disappeared amongst the clouds. Later I stalked a mere speck, which as I had expected turned out to be an HA. He was quite close to his Lines so I got his side of him, and was just about to dive when my engine spluttered and gave up the ghost. Of course I had to come down then and as I was only about a mile the wrong side of the Lines, I knew I should get back. As I passed over I had my pot at the Hun, though at rather long range, and he went puck-puck-puck back at me while I went on down. He made no effort to follow me, so I glided to about 4,000 yards this side of the Lines. As I was landing my undercarriage charged into some rather low telephone wires, which turned me up on my nose. I did no serious damage, and at 3.30 pm I was off again, having been entertained by some Pioneers. When I got off again, of course, I had to give the large crowd a 'farewell', so I played about considerably over their heads. I was very amused to see their stampede on two occasions, as I dived at them, especially to watch the colonel hop out of the way. I climbed up a bit and, after giving them an Immelmann dive, I fluttered off. What amused me greatly at the time was to know that that fat Hun has probably claimed me as a victim, and as having turned up on my nose etc, and I've no doubt their archies corroborated the fact too. What they must have thought when they saw a DH rise from the same spot in the afternoon and fly as if mad for about 15 minutes, I don't know.

Very many thanks for the 'smokes' for my mechanics. My engine man's name is 1st AM Jackson, and my rigger is 1st AM A.M. Davidson. They split them up. I wonder if you could find that thick yellow Jaeger vest of mine; I have asked you for it once or twice; and send it out. A pair of warm *woollen* gloves which come over your wrists would be very acceptable, and also a pair of mittens. A fellow in a neighbouring squadron got frostbite in the air.

32 Squadron RFC. 23 October 1916
It seems to be my luck to have a goodly supply of work to do on Sundays. I don't know why. Perhaps the idea is to keep me out of mischief at least one day in the week. At any rate yesterday I started my day at eight o'clock when I got up, and I didn't finish until I landed back here at dusk. It so happens that just at present we are

living in busy times. The Huns are making the best effort to take over the air supremacy they have made since July, and a lively time they are giving we poor wretched DH pilots who are responsible for keeping them back. So far they are just about where they started. If machines have anything to do with it we all ought to be sitting on our backsides round Bapaume in a couple of days. The poor old DH Scout is becoming more like a 'Longhorn' these days, though it still gets a certain amount of respect.

The Huns always did have very much better machines than ours, though they never thought they were for use. Their sole purpose was to tax their machines to their utmost at running away. And I think as in most things they were pretty successful. But the good days of July and August, when two or three DH's used to push half-a-dozen Huns onto the chimney tops of Bapaume, are no more. In the Roland they possessed the finest two-seater machine in the world, and now they have introduced a few of their single-seater ideas, and very good they are too, one specimen especially deserves mention. They are manned by jolly good pilots, probably the best, and the

Opposition. Line of Albatros D.I Scouts of Jagdstaffel 2 (Boelcke) in October 1916. Nearest pilots, left to right, are Ltn Erwin Böhme, Unknown, Ltn Stephen Kirmaier, and Offstvtr. Max Müller. At this time Jagdstaffel 2 was possibly the elite unit of the German Air Services.

juggling they can do when they are scrapping is quite remarkable. They can fly round and round a DH and make one look quite silly. I haven't had the pleasure at close quarters yet, but if you don't believe *me* you ask Edmund. He knows all about them; his patrol met about a dozen of them the other day, and I think he had a merry time with three or four of them. Most of our fellows have come across them. Aizlewood thoroughly enjoyed himself scrapping three or four the other day when Wallace helped him. Poor old Wallace complained that he never fired a shot at the little brutes, as he could never get his sights on, and he is no contemptible aviator.

Yesterday morning A Flight's patrol (five machines) reported abnormal hostile activity. They reckoned there were about 50 Huns up round Bapaume. However, they fought hard and continuously, and Bonnel pushed one Hun down in a mess, and several others went home with something to think about! The result of all this was that the whole squadron went up in the afternoon, and also met a patrol of Edmund's squadron (24) and between us put some half-dozen Huns in rapid flight, but as a whole the operation was a failure. Corby, who seems bent on putting an end to his sweet life, went down to 1,000 feet after a Hun just alongside a big Hun aerodrome, without attaining his object; and Curphey, thinking that a Hun battery was looking too busy, went down and fired his machine gun at it, as a signal to cease fire. Three of us went down to 3,000 feet after a Roland, without any success, and I felt that was plenty low enough for me! But then I am getting stale and old-fashioned. We have put down two or three other Huns during the week, but really we are getting so blasé about it that I can't for the life of me remember who did the tricks. I feel fairly confident that it wasn't myself.

A great catastrophe has come over us. We have to leave this dear spot where we have striven so successfully to make ourselves comfortable, and move to a beastly place near the Lines. It will be canvas again and everything that is nasty and horrid. Thank goodness we have got a top-hole CO who will soon see us fairly comfortable again. Do you know I have done six – months (in weeks) out here, and that I have had enough. 'I want to go home'. However, I don't seem to have done a fearful lot. I am still a robust Second Lieutenant, and as far as I can see I shall end the war as I started it, or the war will end me. The only remarkable thing I can find about myself is that I have successfully maintained my position as the youngest member of this squadron, which doesn't get me very far.

32 Squadron, RFC, 29 October 1916
What a terrible life this is! As was expected, our move* has taken place, and we have shifted once again. We have really come to a most 'delightful' place, and if anyone wanted really to become thoroughly miserable for any length of time they have only to come here. Of course *we* are not miserable because we know everything will be perfectly comfortable by next July, but for the moment we feel a bit 'sticky'. I thought I had seen some pretty magnificent sights in my life, but I don't think I have ever seen anything to touch this. The whole countryside is a mere bog; for real genuine high-class mud I doubt if our variety can be beaten.

We live in tents and most of us have tent boards, so of course we ought not to grumble. It is a mere detail that everything is covered in a thick film of moisture; after all, I have a perfectly good wick lamp to dry my socks by, and although one's servant does deposit a nice layer of slime on the floor every time he enters, there is nothing to beat a hearty indoor slide, is there? Besides it is nice and soft for the feet when one finally rises in the morning. The tendency is not to get up at all unless the elements decree that one is to freeze aloft. Then one *is* in for it. One has to get outside one's tent then, and that is the end of all things. As soon as a foot is let drop off the tent boards it disappears out of sight. The other foot is then placed in front and likewise conceals itself. The first foot is then salved and if one's overshoes *and* boots are still on, the process is repeated until the 'Mess' is reached. The 'Mess' consists of a large hangar, inside which is a large perfectly good table. This is surrounded by a rather superior type of mud, the rain being cleansed before it falls on it by filtering through the canvas. This is where one sits during the better part of the day and either gambles or waits for the next meal to take place, when one performs the usual exercises.

The walk up to the aerodrome is equally refreshing. The 'drome is at the summit of the slope on which we live; we get there by swimming across the mud roads, struggling along mud paths and fighting through a mud turnip field. When you get near the top you see our transport park, where one usually sees sundry lorries foundering in the mud with their back wheels digging graves for themselves, and a crowd of mechanics shouting and pushing. The

* From Vert Galand to Lealvillers.

aerodrome itself is not so bad and quite spacious; true, it contains a beetroot and a potato patch, but one should be able to avoid these after six months' experience out here. Most of the trenches have been filled up. We share the place with a BE2c squadron, who have settled here some time ago, and have naturally pinched the best places.

I suppose this is a pretty fine grouse, but what would life be like without grousing. As a matter of fact we shall all be under huts in a comparatively short time. In fact all the other officers are building one now under the careful supervision of a corporal; later we shall get tons of cinders, and probably a number of duckboards, and life will be quite bearable. At present everyone is terribly cramped and nothing can be got at. All my stuff is tied up in bags and boxes while I wait for better days.

We had one rather exciting air-scrap two or three days ago. It was a dud day, when three of us, Coleman, King and I, arrived at the Lines at about 6,000 feet. Our first view of them was over the side of a cloud, when at the same moment we caught sight of our artillery machines making for the Lines in great haste, and one below us being severely tackled by two very fast Huns. These were the Hun 'Nieuports' which I have mentioned before as most wonderful machines and flown by the elite of the Hun Flying Corps – Boelcke included I think. There were six of these fellows above, working in pairs.

Down we went for these two low ones, and I did some bad shooting on them as I got near. They are almost too quick to shoot at. The other high ones then came down, and the engagement became general. As far as I was concerned the whole business was a 'whirl' at 3,000 feet over the trenches. I would hear puck-puck-puck behind me and round I would go, sometimes I would see a fellow whirling about 1,000 feet above me on a wing-tip, or I would see nothing at all. We all became separated. Once I caught sight of two little brats at about 1500 flying about 1,000 yards our side of the Lines, thoroughly enjoying themselves, and as pretty a picture as one could wish. They work perfectly together, and can make circles round us. I watched two hawks today chasing another bird – the likeness was remarkable. As I flew just our side of the Lines I noticed one of our BE2c's lying prone across a truck, and another was burning merrily. Unfortunately at the time I thought this second one was a Hun. Coleman struck off in another direction and said he saw two others lying the other side of the Lines, and also claims to have

Alan Vivian Lewis, a first cousin to the author, who joined the RNAS in July 1916 and was killed in a flying accident at the Isle of Grain, September 1918.

brought one of the 'little fellers' down himself. I fear my scrapping is becoming more and more 'windy'. I cannot feel like I did when I came out. I am still hoping they will send we old birds home. I should come out again all right next year, especially if I had a really first class scout. The whole scrap only lasted about five minutes, and then they were off again; in the next minute they seemed to have sprung up about 5,000 feet.

We all take much interest in what is said at home about us, especially by C.G. Grey in the *Aeroplane*. I don't think there is anyone who aggravates us more, unless it is these terrible poses of the 'Zepp-Strafers' which hit one in the eye everytime one picks up a piece of paper. I suppose the real reason is we are jealous; I have no doubt we are. Grey says these 'night birds' are the bravest of all pilots, completely forgetting that 50 per cent of the Flying Corps in the field fly both by day and night over enemy Lines. I wish they would send a few of them out here for a 'holiday' and let us go home and do a little 'work'!! Not many people would object. MP's say much more absurd things, in fact they must be completely mad, especially Major Baird. The trouble is that each fortnight there is a completely different state of affairs out here. The machines change, moral changes, and the fighting becomes more systematic and more cunning. There is nothing resembling the fighting that took place in the second half of July during the present time. Hostile tactics have exactly reversed themselves, and to keep them back we have to change accordingly.

France, 5 November 1916
Just a line to tell you that I have practically got over a slight attack of appendicitis. It came on when I was dining with Edmund. The next day they shifted me to a Field hospital, and today I came to a Casualty Clearing Station where several highly important fellows poked me about and told me the news. I told them I had a similar attack about three months ago, so we decided not to risk a third. Tomorrow I shall go to base and have the brute chopped out. I think it will be a very good idea, as I am just about fed up with this war, only I wish it had happened after leave, which was due this week. The last attack I got over in about three days, so didn't know or think anything more about it. This attack is taking just about the same time. Well, cheerio, and don't worry about me. It will be a nice cheap way of getting the job done.

*Second Lieutenant Edmund Llewelyn Lewis, the author's elder brother.
Edmund joined the army in August 1914, being commissioned in the Essex
Regt, sent to the Middle East and being invalided home at the end of 1915.
Transferring to the RFC in April 1916, he eventually joined his brother on 32
Squadron, was lightly wounded on July 28th and returned to England. In early
October 1916 he again went to France, joining 24 Squadron (DH2's) under the
command of Major Lanoe Hawker, VC, DSO. On December 26th 1916,
Edmund was last seen fighting single-handed against at least five enemy fighters
from Jagdstaffel 'Boelcke', and failed to return. Leutnant Diether Collin of
Jagdstaffel 'Boelcke' was credited with the victory, but was himself killed in
action August 13th 1918.*

LETTER RECEIVED FROM CORPORAL WILLIAM DALTON, RFC

32 Squadron, RFC, Christmas Eve, 1916
Dear Sir,

Really I don't know how to thank you for your great kindness in writing to us as you did. Medals and decorations have little chance of finding their way to the rank and file of the RFC, but personally I am quite content if this war brings me nothing more than your letter. It will be my most treasured 'souvenir' of 'The Great War'. We are all very, very sorry indeed to lose you – nowadays *good* pilots are few and far between – and the news that you are making a good recovery from your regrettable illness is very acceptable to us all. We hope you will soon be able to show them how flying should be done in England, for if the efforts of the new pilots we are getting out now be any criterion, I'm very much afraid flying is only a lost art there now! I came out with No.32 and so I think I am entitled to pass an opinion on it; my opinion is, sir, that it reached its zenith about September 1916, and it is now a wash-out. Within the last week we have lost three machines, not in actual service but in *school* flying. Poor old 32!

Since you left us, sir, everything has been one big mix-up. Lt Corbett took over '7888'; he was a game pilot and a gallant gentleman, but inexperienced. Within a week he crashed her. Exit '7888'. I wonder if inanimate objects have feelings; did she miss the master-touch that had controlled her for so long? Who can say? He got another machine, did a few flights in it and went over the line – never to return! Captain Nicholas, Lts Coleman, King and he went on a patrol – King flying a B Flight bus – and encountered a strong Hun patrol. King had bad engine trouble – B Flight again – and was out of the running all the time, and the last that was seen of Lt Corbett was his bus diving hell for leather, with a Hun on his tail. I do not know whether he lives yet or no; if not, he is one more good man lost.[22] Captain Henty followed you to hospital very soon, and is 'struck-off'. Lt Hunt took over his place as Flight commander of B Flight – and lasted a week! He had an arrangement of double guns – two guns instead of one – on his bus, and on his first trip over he failed to return. Isn't war a hellish business?[23]

Mechanics are human beings, *very* human sometimes, and it is awful for them to see these men, good and true gentlemen in the true sense of the word, going off with a 'Cheerio' never to return. My nerve was as steady as a rock until I saw Lt Bentley killed at Vert Galand – I held him down in his death agony – and since then it has not been worth a damn.[24] Lt King, Capt Jones and Lt Maremontemboult have all had crashes since you left ('Monty', as he was affectionately called, smashing his sixth bus, and incidentally being struck off, wounded). Just to give you an idea of the type of pilots we are getting; one day this week four pilots in A Flight pulled out a machine and put a new pilot in it. He was perfectly game, although he had never flown a De Hav. before. He did a few circuits and missed the aerodrome twice in landing. He must have lost his head completely then, for he landed *with* the wind, and crashed. B Flight wrecked another today, on the aerodrome. It is sad. Lt Coleman is posted to Home Establishment and left us at the beginning of the week. I believe Captain Nicholas follows suit in a few weeks' time. What will become of us then?

So much for the officers and machines, now a word or two as to the men. Sergeant Saunders went to hospital and I have taken his place in the workshops. One of the Flight men went to hospital with some mysterious disease – rumour says 'spotted fever' – anyway, the remainder of the men who slept in his billet, including Jackson and Davidson, were at once isolated. Within a week Jackson and Falconer, the carpenter, followed suit, and are now struck off. I called Davidson to the window of his hut and told him of your letter. He wishes me to thank you for him, and asks if you still have a certain negative which was exposed at Vert Galand. We would dearly like a momento of '7888'. I don't think there is much more to tell, sir; I only hope that I have not wearied you with this rambling epistle. The boys all join me in wishing you the very best of luck, and we will keep our eyes on the Honours Lists, for you cannot hide your light under a bushel for ever.

Yours obediently,
(Corporal) Chas Wm Dalton.

Notes to Part I

[1] Alfred de Bathe Brandon, a New Zealander, qualified for his pilot's 'ticket' on 17 October 1915. Joining the RFC in late 1915, he received his Service 'wings' on 26 February 1916. Joining No.39 (Home Defence) Squadron at Hainault Farm, Essex, he attacked the German airship L.15 on the night of March 31, and the Zeppelin, also hit by anti-aircraft gunfire, was forced down in the Thames Estuary. On the night of 23 September 1916, he engaged another raiding airship, the L.33. Damaged by Brandon's attack, and AA fire, the airship force-landed at Little Wigborough, Essex, where its crew set fire to their ship and then surrendered themselves to local authorities.

[2] Charles G. Grey first came into aviation journalism at the turn of the century, and became joint editor of *The Aero*, a one penny weekly, from May 1909 until the paper's demise in 1911. Later that year he was approached by E.V. Sassoon (later, Sir Victor Sassoon, Bart) who provided the initial finance for creation of a new weekly aviation magazine, *The Aeroplane*, the first issue of which appeared in June 1911 with Grey as editor; a position he held until 1939. A staunch advocate of British aviation, he was renowned for his blunt, outspoken criticism of bureaucracy in any form, but particularly in regard to matters affecting British military aviation. Grey once remarked, 'I never minded making enemies. The scriptures enjoin us to love our enemies; I loved mine so much that I made a hobby of collecting them.' He died on 9 December 1953.

[3] Lieutenant Maurice Duncan Basden, 27 Squadron RFC, was killed in action flying Martinsyde G.100, 7278, on 20 May 1916.

[4] Captain Henry Arthur Taylor, MC, 27 Squadron, was killed in combat on 27 September 1916, by Hauptmann Oswald Boelcke, leader of the German Jagdstaffel 2; Boelcke's 29th accredited victory. Taylor was 18 years old.

[5] 'Archie' was the soubriquet commonly applied by all RFC and RNAS air crews to the German anti-aircraft guns. It derived from a contemporary music hall catchphrase, 'Archibald, certainly not!

[6] Second Lieutenant Reginald A. Stubbs was killed on 8 June 1916, flying DH2,6005.

[7] Second Lieutenant William Eric Nixon was wounded in combat on 18 June 1916, flying DH2,5983. Rising to Captain, he was wounded twice more in action, and was eventually killed in combat on 7 May 1917.

[8] Major Lionel Wilmot Brabazon Rees, MC, commander of 32 Squadron, was awarded a Victoria Cross for this action, which took place on 1 July 1916, the opening day of the First Battle of the Somme. A Welshman, Rees entered the Royal Garrison Artillery in December 1903, and transferred to the RFC in August 1914. Awarded a Military Cross for his outstanding work with 11 Squadron in France in

1915, he then became the first CO of 32 Squadron on its formation. He remained in the RAF after the war, retiring in 1931 as Group Captain, VC, OBE, MC, AFC, and died on 28 September 1955.

[9] Oberleutnant Max Immelmann, the so-termed 'Eagle of Lille', was killed during a combat with FE2b's of No. 25 Squadron RFC on 18 June 1916. The RFC credited his death to the crew of FE2b,6346, piloted by Second Lieutenant G.R. McCubbin and his gunner Corporal J. Waller, but German records generally insist that his death was due to structural failure in Immelmann's Fokker E.III machine, which broke up in the air.

[10] Tom Alger Elliott Cairnes first saw operational service as an Observer with 15 Squadron RFC in France in 1915. Qualifying as a pilot at Norwich, he was then posted as a Flight commander to the newly-formed 27 Squadron and went to France with the unit in March 1916. Promoted to command 32 Squadron, he ended the war as Lieutenant-Colonel, DSO, in command of the 22nd (Army) Wing – all this despite the fact that he possessed only one eye, the consequence of a polo accident some years before the war.

[11] Sidney Dalrymple was one of the original pilots of 27 Squadron RFC when it first flew to France, March 1916. By 1918 he was a Captain serving with 139 Squadron RAF (Bristol F2b's) on the Italian front.

[12] Second Lieutenant John Godlee crashed in DH2,7874, near Noeux Les Mines on 19 July 1916, and died of his injuries and wounds on 22 July.

[13] Sergeant Eric Henry Dobson first qualified for his pilot's certificate (as a Corporal) on 13 August 1915. He was shot down in flames, flying DH2,6015, near Faucourt L'Abbaye on 12 August 1916.

[14] Second Lieutenant Eric Fothergill Bainbridge, flying DH2,7916, was lost in action on 5 September 1916, being last seen spinning down out of control after a combat over Delville Wood.

[15] Captain Robert E. Wilson, flying DH2,7895, was shot down on 2 September 1916 by Hauptmann Oswald Boelcke, who was flying Fokker D III,352/16. It was Boelcke's 20th accredited victory and the first for his newly-formed Jagdstaffel 2, based then at Bertincourt. Despite the completely riddled condition of his DH2, Wilson effected a reasonable landing and managed to get out of the machine just as it burst into flames. He was entertained by Boelcke the following day, prior to entering a prisoner of war camp.

[16] A reference to Lieutenant William Leefe Robinson, VC who was awarded his Victoria Cross for his destruction of the German airship SL.11 on the night of 2 September 1916 – the first such victory over English soil. On 5 April 1917, when a Captain with 48 Squadron in France, Robinson was shot down in Bristol F2a,A3337 by Vizefeldwebel Sebastian Festner of Jagdstaffel 11, and became a prisoner of war. Repatriated to England in December 1918, Robinson died of influenza on 31 December 1918. His grave may be seen today at All Saints Cemetery, Harrow Weald, Middlesex.

[17] Second Lieutenant G. Greenwood Bentley, in DH2,A2553, was killed on 17 September 1916, while trying to make a turn with a failing engine. The machine side-slipped and nose-dived into the ground.

[18] *In the Royal Naval Air Service*, by Flight Lieutenant Harold Rosher, RN, published by Chatto and Windus, 1916 – a collection of letters to Rosher's family written during the author's service with No. 1 Wing, RNAS up until his death in a flying accident at Dover on 27 February 1916.

[19] Captain Herman W von Poellnitz, MC who gained his Royal Aero Club

Certificate No.1953 on 26 October 1915.

[20] Leutnant Kurt Wintgens, who achieved historical fame as the first German pilot to destroy an enemy aircraft using a Fokker M5 monoplane fitted with a synchronised machine gun, when he shot down a French Morane on 1 July 1915. He subsequently received the *Ordre Pour Le Merite* (the so-called 'Blue Max') and amassed 18 accredited victories before his death on 25 September 1916.

[21] See Note 4. The other 27 Squadron loss in this same combat was Second Lieutenant Stephen Dendrino, in Martinsyde G.100,7495, who also fell to the guns of Hauptmann Oswald Boelcke. A subsequent claim for the death of Dendrino was made by Vizefeldwebel Rudolf Reimann of Boelcke's Jagdstaffel 2; the victory was therefore simply credited to the unit, and not to an individual pilot.

[22] Lieutenant Roland Corbett, in DH2,A2607, was shot down on 22 November 1916 by Leutnant Erich König of Jagdstaffel 2 ('Boelcke'), König's second accredited victory.

[23] Lieutenant P.B.G. Hunt was shot down in DH2,5986 on 11 December 1916 by Leutnant (later, Rittmeister) Manfred Freiherr von Richthofen. Hunt was wounded but survived to become a prisoner of war.

[24] See Note 17.

PART II

1917-1918

Central Flying School
Upavon
Wiltshire
17 June 1917

Central Flying School, Upavon, Wiltshire. 17 June 1917

I am really living a most awful life here. I am what is known as an 'Assistant Instructor'. I exist for the general benefit of the Flight commander. When I first arrived the Flight commander of my Flight was under orders to leave the next day, so I stepped straight into his job, and learnt it as quickly as I could. That was quite good fun though rather hard work for one instructor. Of course, I must start by pointing out that I had to get up at about 4.30 am every morning (the weather being always fine) and finishing about 9 pm in the evening. However, as you can probably guess, it was only the getting up that worried me.

The pupils I get are people who have been through elementary instruction though Heaven knows they are still elementary enough. At any rate I have no dual control to do, which is a great blessing. The machines are BE2e's with 90hp RAF (engine), and BE12's with 140hp RAF and a single seat. My great difficulty at first was to put myself back 18 months, and remember exactly what my feelings were at the time. I was always forgetting about wind and bumps and their effect on the beginner. However, I am showing signs of improvement! It is remarkable what a crowd of silly information one has to impart to a 'Hun' (pupil) before he starts, no matter what he is doing.

The whole course here is perfectly excellent now, being entirely progressive. The organisation is also very good. Instructors are continually seeking for talent which is lamentably scarce. The best pilots we send on to fly scouts. Sometimes they are returned as not good enough, as the standard for scouts is necessarily high. Others which fail to fly scouts are selected for fast two-seaters. The worst are kept for artillery machines, and one here and there is fired out for being 'too expensive'. However, that is very seldom. The training is also very good. Artillery pilots are all taught how to control a 'shoot' by ground practice and also from the air with smoke puffs and

Scottish warrior. A DH2 (unarmed) being prepared for a training flight at the School of Air Fighting at Loch Doon, Ayr, 1917. The author served at this unit, as an instructor, during early 1917.

wireless, how to take photos and drop bombs. Previously they had to learn it in France. Likewise, scout pilots are taught how to do trick flying of all kinds, and also how to fight. There are also various other tests to complete, and I spend most of my time crashing these poor fellows into the air and testing their machines. We also do a daily practice flight in formation, and I remember leading them over Marlborough at about 5,000 feet. We do the formation flying in the BE12's. It is quite astounding how bad some of these people can be. As in all branches of the Service, the standard of officer is rather low, and it is remarkable how one picks the gentlemanly fellow for the faster machines.

A new Flight commander has now turned up which somewhat robs me of my control. However I knew what I was in for when I took the job. Strangely enough he was a 'Hun' at Netheravon when I went out with No.32. He has been in France a considerable time as an artillery pilot, and naturally adapts himself to the types of machine in the Flight. Personally, I can't stick them, as I haven't got enough muscle to control them. The 'Huns' down here are quite terrifying at times. They will insist on saluting me and calling me 'Sir' and all these other nasty things. It doesn't seem to worry them that I bounce about twice as high as any of them landing. One poor fellow broke a wire landing the other day, and came up to me in a most pitiful condition, tears streaming down his face, and looking quite haggard and worn. He couldn't make it out at all when I roared with laughter at him, and sort of told him to be a good boy and go home, and promised not to tell his mother! We don't encourage stupidity though. This was all when I was more or less independent; now I have to try to make myself into a nice subordinate. Allen is quite nice as squadron CO.

Yesterday I took a fellow called C.N. Jones, an OM, over to Marlborough in a BE2e. We sort of fell into the school grounds, and I had lunch with Emery while he went into 'Hall'. I nearly put an end to my sweet life taking off again, trying to push some trees down, and also jolly nearly swept the steeple off the church! However, I still live to tell the tale. Fortunately we landed without many people knowing, so the machine remained more or less intact.

BE2e, No.6669 – an example of the type of machine flown by the author whilst at CFS, Upavon during mid-1917.

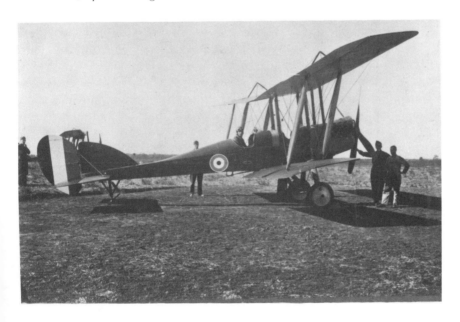

CFS, Upavon, Wilts. 24 June 1917

There has been a distinct change in the weather during the last week. It has been mostly cloudy with strong winds blowing and occasional rain. Aviation, as a result, has not been so prosperous, but the pupils I get are more or less in an advanced stage, so we have got a fair amount of work done. It is good for them to get bumped about well, so long as they perch their kite intact. Barring a few broken wires, strained struts and undercarriages, all has been fairly well. When I see a 'Hun' showing a little spirit and keenness in aviation, I take him up in a dual control machine and expound the theory of vertical turns, stalls, spirals, etc and then persuade him to do a few himself. This morning a fellow sideslipped me 1500 feet before I knew where I was! I couldn't quite grasp why the clouds were suddenly above me, when I knew a few moments before I was well above them. Of course, we slipped through a gap.

Lord Derby had a glance at us during the week. There was all sorts of hot air floating about; machines lined up and everyone to be very punctual etc. I dropped rather a brick by rolling up late, only half-awake and all bleary-eyed. Of course I had slept too long. I am afraid I suffered the severe displeasure of my squadron commander, especially as I was in charge of the Flight at the time. It rather tickled me after all the hot air had been distributed, though I certainly felt ashamed of myself. I don't suppose I had been late for any show for months and months, and of course it isn't very good for my 'Huns'. However, Derby soon got fed-up as it was a dud day.

The school is now swarming with gibbering Russians. Most trying for the nerves! So far I haven't got any of them as they are not advanced enough. I have got two Norwegians though, and very good fellows they are. They are two of the five officers in the Norwegian Flying Corps, and as we have sold Norway some machines they are being allowed to fly our best, and also to learn all our methods of instruction. They are taking the full course here, and it is pretty full too compared with what it was in my time. They now give pilots a little training before they go out instead of letting them train themselves when they get overseas. Personally I think these fellows are very privileged.

CFS, Upavon, Wilts. 2 July 1917

Captain H.W.G. Jones and von Poellnitz have arrived here in various capacities, thus adding to the happy gathering of No.32.

Jones and I decided we wanted to do something yesterday afternoon, so I had an old BE2e pushed out, and set out for Eastbourne in a howling gale. Fortunately the machine could be fitted up with dual control if necessary, so I warned Jones to be ready if I fainted or anything comic. There was such a strong wind blowing that it took us $2\frac{1}{2}$ hours to get there, which was longer than we had expected, and only just left us time for tea at the 'Grand' when we got there!

We landed at an RNAS aerodrome, where they were very good to us. The sun was shining nicely on the outward journey, so I struck the coast at Bognor and from there flew along the shore at about 100 feet. It was really quite refreshing to see everyone carrying on as if it were summer, bathing, digging and messing about on piers etc. We carried on in the same way past Worthing, Shoreham, Brighton, Seaford and Eastbourne, being bumped to blazes the whole time. We did the same thing coming home again and really had quite an amusing though rather tedious journey. Several times it struck me we should look rather stupid if the engine had conked, but fortunately it had the grace not to, though it seriously over-heated once. It was the famous 90 hp RAF!

During the week I was teaching a 'Hun' how to stunt a bit when I found myself over Marlborough, so perched on the Common for a few minutes.

CFS, Upavon, Wilts. 7 August 1917
I have just time to write a few lines before the weather clears; there is a thick mist at present. Captain Allen has got a Home Defence squadron, I know not where, but probably outside London, so he has left us.[1] Captain Jones, whose name you also know, has taken command of the squadron, probably temporarily, and so has vacated the SE5 Flight. I have stepped into that, at any rate for the time being. These fellows have all been very good to me. Allen did what he could, and Jones especially asked the Commandant that I should take over his Flight. Jones has now heard that he is not going to get the squadron, so perhaps he will take over again, though he says he is going to do his best to leave me here.

It is good fun having one's own little show to run. I have an excellent Flight Sergeant, which is the best of good luck, so I can spend most of my time on the pupils. I think it is the only training Flight in the country, or one of very few, and consequently the hot air coming through from above is nearly stifling. Yesterday two

CFS, Upavon, 1917. At left is Gerald Allen, an ex-member of 32 Squadron during the author's service on the unit; while the author relaxes in the foreground.

telegrams came through, each demanding five more SE pilots. I gave them *one*! I just carry on, and fly when the weather is fine. There are two SE5's, one with the 150 hp and the other with 200 hp. I had two 150's which I have to start the pupils on, one was going well, and it was fully time to take the other's engine down – a three days' job. Of course, someone crashed the good one last night, good and hearty, and now the other one is no good, so how am I going to turn out these brilliant (?) pilots for them!! Just my luck! However, it is rather comic. The fellow who tried to ruin my career for me won't trouble me again. He has rather spoilt his good looks and is now lying in Tidworth Hospital. Lucky he isn't strawberry jam! All through landing with his tail up. Probably do it myself soon. I have quite a hearty loathing for this machine, though only on the quiet. It is too heavy and turns too slowly. A Sopwith Camel for me!

On Sunday about 15 of us flew over to the Public Schools camp and had great fun. Luckily the wind was blowing in the right direction, so we all perched our kites safely. Two of our fellows gave these boys as wonderful an exhibition of flying as is possible at a very low altitude, and also had a sham fight. I saw Herbert but they wouldn't let me take him up. Also Colonel Wall in great form, shouting through his teeth! Later, I flew off and had tea with another fellow's friends, and returned in the rain.

CFS, Upavon, Wilts. 12 August 1917

I have been living a most terrible life lately, though a life really very full of interest to me. I am still running the SE Flight which, funnily enough, is the most conspicuous in the school at present, and probably in the country. What I mean is that I have an enormous order for pilots before the end of the month, and the Commandant is naturally anxious to get them trained from his point of view, and the Air Board look on to see their casualties are filled up etc, and I like the job and want to keep it. My worst trouble has been the weather, which has not been very kind. The machines have gone fairly well, and I have fetched two new ones from Farnborough, so I have partially got over the two crashes I had to start with.

I get up every morning at 5 am and seldom leave the sheds until 8.30 pm, so I don't get too much spare time. The mechanics have had to put in more time than ever before, so they naturally hate me. However, they will get over that as they get used to me, and as I get to know more about my job I shall fuss less. It is difficult not to fuss when the Commandant comes round every day and frightens me by knowing nearly as much about my pupils as I do myself, and the Assistant Commandant appears at least twice daily, and asks me the names of people in the machines, and I can never remember them! When he does that I always produce a bunch of photographs of Loch Doon, and that always keeps him quite! On the whole I am getting to like the SE very much better myself, though it is rather heavy and slow manoeuvring. As a rule I don't get much time to fly myself. Scouts are now divided into two classes, Stationary Scouts and Rotary Scouts.

CFS, Upavon, Wilts. 1 September 1917

At the beginning of the month everything went well, and I started turning out promising young aviators like a mincing machine. Then suddenly everything went wrong. All the machines went dud, and nothing on earth would make them 'marche'. I had a selection of bad 'Huns' who smashed them for me, and oil tanks, radiators etc burst by numbers, until suddenly I found myself with half a serviceable machine, where I had calculated on five. Well, something had to be done, so I put my hand to my enormously brainy forehead, and with the help of my nearly equally brainy senior fitter, we solved the oil problem. Then we, or perhaps I should say, some of the men, spent the whole night hammering engines into their correct shape, and I fear have spent several since!

Things still went very badly so I decided I must have more men. I had a look round and brought to mind that my squadron commander was generated from the same squadron as I was, so I made up to him, and had the other two Flights bled of men, to my own advantage. Even then things weren't good enough; I seemed to be up against the devil himself. The radiators took into their heads to leak as soon as we opened throttles; I had four radiators leak in my three only serviceable machines in one day, and that was a bit too thick. It takes a *good* man four hours to change a radiator, and a bad one about a day. The result was a large splash was made about radiators, and the situation has now somewhat improved, though there are still a few oaths in my speech when it refers to radiators. The dud weather of this last half month has more or less saved us; the other day I saw six perfectly good machines standing in my hangar, so I said 'Good enough' and started thinking about leave.

Six machines were too much for the devil to look at though! One of my perfectly good pilots took up a kite, went round in small circles, and then pushed it into the side of a valley, spreading strawberry jam in all directions. Funnily enough he is still alive, and I hope likely to remain so, though I was very annoyed with him at the time. He had flown them quite well before, and he was too good a fellow to waste like that, let alone a battle-kite. This was the final effort necessary to send me on leave, and a hurried application was put in for 48 hours.

I seemed to spend most of my time in the RA Club telephoning to Vincent, without any success. I then went and had supper with the Carpenters, and we decided with one accord that we would like to dance. So M –, T –, Mrs C – and I went to Oxford Street to dance. I also ran headlong into Cairnes, who was on leave, and fed with him, along with two other majors and another comic fellow. It was great fun and I told him I would go out to him tomorrow if he would only get a respectable machine. They have got a thing called a DH5 which is not good enough in these hard times.

The next bit of information is that tomorrow I am going down to Gosport for a course of stunt flying or something equally amusing. I shall be there two or three weeks, I am not sure which.

Fort Grange, Gosport. 10 September 1917

I am afraid I rather misunderstood what I was coming here for, and consequently seem to have rather frightened you. What really happens here is super instruction. Some clever people down here have devised a very sound system of instruction, and to standardize this in the Flying Corps they train other instructors. It is mostly for dual control. They have got at the theory of the whole thing and instead of flying in the slip-shod fashion that most of us taught ourselves to do, you learn exactly what you are doing, and why you do it, and so can teach others the same sort of thing.

The amusing part of the show is that many others like myself have found out how very badly they really fly, and have settled down to learn again, under the supervision of very critical instructors. Of course there are a number of little tricks thrown in, which were once thought clever, because we knew how to do them without knowing what we were doing, and consequently flying far from perfectly. Some misguided individuals come down here feeling proud, but one can only feel sorry for them. However good you are, you are nearly sure to learn something on a show like this. In fact one individual considered by many the best pilot in the Corps, said that he learnt more about flying in three weeks down here than in the three years previous.

I must thank you all very much for your hearty congratulations on my third 'pip'. September 10 seems to be my lucky day. All my pips have been awarded on that day! More than one of the people learning to fly with me are now majors and really I seem to have more seniority in the Corps than five out of six Flight commanders I meet. However, that is no matter now, and you will be pleased to know that your telegram was the first definite news I had on the subject.

CFS, Upavon, Wilts. 9 October 1917

After I returned from leave I had a tremendous pressure of work. I turned out about 10 pretty good pilots in a very few days, and I can tell you I had very little rest from morn to night. The last day I passed four fellows out in Fighting, two in camera gun work, and lead two formations, as well as the ordinary duties of running the Flight and getting people off on their first solos, and begging them not to crash! On the whole I was very lucky. In other words, unlike the previous month, my luck was in!

On last Tuesday some of these fellows still hadn't gone overseas, so I decided that I felt like a cross-country formation. By a tremendous stroke of luck, I found that practically all my kites were serviceable. I therefore had nine of them lined up, stuck in eight other pilots, and crashed off in what was supposed to be a 'formation' to Shoreham. It was pretty dud when we started, but we climbed above the first layer of clouds and got to about 7,000 feet. We then came down low and showed ourselves to Brighton before landing. To our amazement we found while landing that there was a perfect gale blowing, and we were thrown about in a most merciless manner. I jolly near crashed myself; only saved myself by inches. Sort of chasing along the ground, praying for flying speed before my wing-tip touched! However, we all got down safely except one, who turned over. That wasn't at all bad under the circumstances.

The next question was whether it was good enough to go back or whether the risk was too great. I was very nervous as to what Commandants and people might think, but finally decided to stay. The OC down there wasn't too friendly, so I left him alone and carried on without his help. He told me he had room for two machines in the hangars, and the others would have to be pegged down outside. However, he was surprised to see a short time later that there were none outside. We, of course, had to retire to Brighton for the night. The place was very full. However we got put up in some funny places, and even the Commander had to share a bed with another fellow. The next day there was a perfect gale blowing, so returning was out of the question. I think I spent most of the day quietening my nerves in the barber's shop.

The next morning was fine but fairly breezy. As usual we were up at daybreak, and eight of us crashed off together. This time the formation was better. We flew for about an hour and a quarter, and had just passed Chichester, when my engine gave a splutter, and fire and black smoke started to stream out of the exhaust pipes. The others thought I was on fire; the carburetter certainly was. Again my luck was in; I had noticed a good field a few miles back. By turning down-wind I managed to just make it and land safely. Then the comic show started! The 'Huns' thought 'Halloo', here goes our commander, we must follow' and hanged if they didn't all perch alongside me. Unfortunately the whole show was spoilt by the same silly ass turning over another machine. This time I was *annoyed*!

The progress had been alarmingly slow, considering our air speed had been 90 mph, so I decided they must wait for petrol, as there was a risk that they might *just* run out. Again I was rather nervous, as it was a lively day. The petrol didn't come till late, so I decided on an early start. I had fitted a new carburetter by this time. What was my horror when I woke up next morning before daybreak, and heard the rain simply sheeting down. The machines, of course, were out in the open this time. At about 10.30 the rain stopped, and I went up to test the air. The clouds had risen to 1500 feet so I decided to make the effort. All that was left of us therefore crashed off, and all seven of us perched safely this time at CFS. Well, now you see why my letters have been delayed so!

40 Squadron, RFC, BEF France. 10 December 1917, (Bruay)
Just a few lines to let you know my address, and to tell you I have reached this land of sunshine and promise intact, and more or less in my right mind. The crossing was quite nice; rather cold and wet, but an escort of three destroyers gave one a sense of security. At Boulogne I found a tender waiting. Seven officers and much kit strode into the tender and partook of one of the most miserably cold journeys I have ever experienced. After nearly five hours of hard going I was told it was time to get out, and I was surprised to find that I wasn't quite frozen to my seat. I was quite please to hear I was posted to No.40 Squadron. They are a very good bunch of fellows, and Major Tilney is at their head. Father will remember him as I think he once gave him a joyride at the CFS.

The Huns apparently fly out here as well as in England. They have just dropped half-a-dozen eggs round us. I suppose they are meant for the aerodrome; by the sound, they have missed. Oh! there they go again. Much clatter of machine guns so they must be low. Some silly fool has started the machine gun on the aerodrome. You would be amused to see all the people here. About eight of us are in a tin hut, sitting round a very comfortable fire. Some are reading and puffing pipes, others are talking and making noises, another fellow is playing with a pup, while another (dare I say it?) is making a violin squeal (that doesn't mean to say you are to send mine out!) People let fly some nasty language with reference to the Huns, but apparently the fire is too comfortable to move from. The dog still plays and the violin still squeals! This squadron had Nieuports until about six weeks ago when they changed over to SE5's. Most of them seem to prefer their Nieuports, with their quick manoeuvre, to the better performing SE5's. They are all very keen and all out for a scrap.

There is one particularly bright Flight commander here with a bar to his MC. He is the only Flight commander here at present. The others have gone home.

The position of the aerodrome is about half-way between my original aerodrome when I first came out, and the one we went to later. Not a bad front really. I have got hold of quite a good machine, but with my usual keenness I haven't flown it yet. Scared of crashing it landing!

Thanks so much for all coming to see me off. Awfully sorry I decided to come now. It's beastly cold. No need to open the window in my Armstrong hut!

17 December 1917
For your information and necessary action my present location is Bruay, behind Arras and Lens.

40 Squadron, RFC. 19 December 1917
At present we don't do much else except high flying in this squadron, which I am sure will please Dad! Consequently there hasn't been much doing for us over the Lines. A short time ago there was a fine morning and we did two Huns down. Three of our people fell across four Albatros Scouts east of Douai and gave them the fright of their lives. One painted sky blue will rise no more! My engine would not function at the right moment, so I did not get away 'til after the patrol. I therefore went up and had a look round by myself, so as to try and get accustomed to the look of things.

I got up to 16,500 feet when a beastly two-seater Hun insisted on coming in my direction. I simply *had* to *see* him, much as I was dying not to. Of course I made a mess of things as usual. I had to wait to see his markings before I fired, and by that time his nose had started to go down. I made a mighty lunge round and pushed at everything I could in a wild frenzy of excitement. Unfortunately I left my engine full on during my headlong flight, and it soon ceased to function in an orderly manner. By that time I had blazed off a drum from my Lewis gun, but to my great annoyance my Vickers refused to 'marche'. This was later accounted for owing to my not having loaded it! (Don't you dare to tell anyone else!) Anyway the Hun would not stop one of my bullets and went home.

Major Edward Mannock, DSO, MC, the acknowledged top-scoring fighter 'ace' (73 victories) on the Allied side, who was killed in action July 26th 1918, and awarded a posthumous Victoria Cross in 1919. This photo was taken at Hendon when Mannock was receiving pilot training.

The front seems to be very active. The Hun has got so many guns and men, he doesn't know what to do with them all. He seems to be shelling like blazes, and beastly big stuff too by the sound of it. I suppose it is all that keeps the wretched devils in the Line warm. It has been snowing here the last few days. Coal and wood is appallingly short out here this winter, which is rather a jar. I keep warm by putting on so many vests and things that I look like a bally balloon walking about. I think I have got quite a good Flight. One of the fellows is very good. So far it has been rather amusing; everything has gone wrong when it shouldn't! When one patrol was getting away I saw enough to court-martial three men. I hope things will get better now, as we get to know one another better.

I think I told you that we have got an expert Hun-strafer here. Captain Mannock, MC and bar; someone said he had got 17 Huns. Anyway he strafes about on his own, and seems to enjoy himself fairly well. I believe he will be going home soon though. He is an excellent fellow.[2] The Hun still seems very keen on throwing a few eggs every evening. He usually comes fairly early and gets the job off his chest. Except that the lights always go out he hasn't done *us* much damage yet. There are plenty of good targets in this neighbourhood.

40 Squadron, RFC. 23 December 1917
I think I shall miss the post, but this you must put down to the Huns; they have only just finished their usual bomb raid, the worst part of which is that the lights are all put out (our lights are electric and worked from the town). Of course I suppose we could get candles and get on with the work by that means, but you can imagine what happens. It is fairly freezing outside and everyone sits round the fire.

Well, I hope you all have a very bon Christmas. For myself you need have little fear. We are *the lads*, and we shall, of course, have a time a thousand times more gay than you will. It takes one officer all his time to provide sufficient fodder to do justice to the occasion. I suppose there is no harm in having a bit of a fill-out on Christmas Day. Our padre says he sees no reason why everyone should not get thoroughly tight! He is a splendid fellow.[3] Oh! I nearly forgot to tell you my contribution to your Christmas festivities. A day or two ago I fetched down a Hun. I went out with Flight commander Tudhope[4] and one other. He led me a dickens of a march all over the Lines and then spotted four Albatri miles away. Off he went and somehow we

Captain J H Tudhope, MC, a close friend of the author's in 40 Squadron,
1918, a Flight Commander when the author joined the Squadron.

overhauled them by losing height. Down he went on one, fired, and down went the Hun, scared to death and probably hit. Frightened out of my life I thought I had better do something. So off I went after another, and hanged if the beggar didn't turn on me. I dived at him and he zoomed at me. He had me cold, but couldn't shoot straight or something. I just managed to miss crashing into him by pulling up with a tremendous jerk! In fact I was so certain that I had crashed into him that I couldn't collect myself sufficiently to look round. Tudhope said the fellow stalled, fell, wobbled and fell into a spin. He gave it a parting shot.

Of course it won't be confirmed from the ground as it was too far over, so won't count properly as brought down, but only out of control. Anyway, he missed me so Cheer O! Today I had a two-seater cold, about 1500 feet over the trenches. I missed and my engine stopped temporarily, so I had to withdraw. I am afraid it must have looked a very dud show from below.

This is a very cold spot at present. It is more horrid than ever getting up in the morning, to find your sponge, shaving brush and washing materials frozen stiff. However, Mother will be pleased to know that I have been driven to her water bottle! And I also use bed socks! I know one fellow who slept in his flying suit. I have been issued with a perfectly priceless flying suit out here. All in one piece from top to bottom and nicely lined. I believe it is warmer on the ground than in the air!

PS: Major McCloughry arrived here with his squadron a day or two ago.[5] I like him most awfully and some of his men. They are quite a stout lot and very easily made at home. At present it is very difficult to get near our own fire, and the fellows in No.40 are getting rather scared that the supply of liquid that the whole of northern France was searched for, for Christmas festivities is nearly exhausted. Also our cost of living is very high already, and we only have a limited amount of food. This doesn't seem to appeal to them, or that there is a very nice hotel in the town. We can manage a meal or two and don't mind waiting for our own while they feed, but there is a limit to most things! However, I hope it may pay later on as we shall probably work together.

40 Squadron, RFC. 30 December 1917
You all seem to have had a pretty 'bon' Christmas, which is as it should be. I did too, but it is such ages ago since it happened that it

Camel King – Major W A McCloughry, MC, commander of No. 4 Squadron, Australian Flying Corps, at Bruay airfield, 1918. Standing in front of one of his unit's Sopwith F.1 Camel fighters.

has become rather a blur. Some of it is rather a blur for other reasons! Anyway, the great thing was that on our part of the front it was a pretty dud day, and we decided that for once we would give the Huns first chance, and if they became active we would become active too. However, they had the sense not to, so we contented ourselves with mildly exercising our machines. Our schemes for our Christmas dinner were deep and of long preparation, so I decided to spend what time I could in getting into training for the aforementioned function. I therefore strutted off for a long walk, which helped things considerably.

From eventide everything became noisy. I remember I went down to the men's Mess and found them hard at work with a very excellent meal. The officers of each Flight had somewhat contributed towards the success of this in so far as we had done our best to place them all in a complete state of inebriation, and then give them smoker's throat! We obtained some measure of success! An interesting feature of this meal was that the waiters consisted of sergeants and in many cases officers. It was all very noisy. I then prepared for my own dinner. I first put on my oldest clothes. Having been told a few days before by the army chaplain how we ought to spend Christmas, proceeded to do exactly the opposite! Our meal was sumptuous; of course turkey and sticky pudding were the backbone of the whole show, but there were all sorts of other things flying about. I sat down with a fixed determination to consume everything I could lay lands on. In this respect I was successful – the result is on my week's Mess bill.

Anyway the whole show was noisy, In fact I think the Major found me rather troublesome. It was the first time anyone had heard me make any noise. They were all so convinced that I was totally incapable of making my mouth twitter that they have called me 'Noisy'. For once I was not trying to edge near the one and only glimmer of heat, listening or not as the case may be to other people's twittering!

After this horrible orgy the officers en bloc proceeded to the men's quarters again, and then took place what was called a 'concert'. Sometimes it was and sometimes it wasn't. When it wasn't, it developed into a sort of competitive noise between officers and men, the Major spending his time vainly striving to keep irresponsible young officers in order, with only moderate success. The climax was reached when he had a brain-wave and decided to unite officers and men by having an inter-Flight singing competition; the audience to be the judges. Rather a doubtful procedure! Needless to say this led to more noise, and as the audience was in the majority they were able to make more noise than the competing Flight. The whole thing more or less developed into a sort of free scramble, with the result that 'The King' was struck up and the meeting hastily brought to a close. So that was the end of the noise.

When we emerged into the open again there was quite a heavy fall of snow, leading to more promiscuous warfare and noise. I distinctly remember our first victim was a motor-cyclist, who ended up in a ditch. He dismounted, strode up to me and became distinctly noisy. Then the Brigade had to be raided and another concert party snow-balled during their show. Then a flying visit down the streets. And so the evening, or should I say night, went on. I also remember very nearly having a big row with a burly Scotch youth, whose humour I failed to appreciate. However, with the help of many others this was averted. By the time I had subsided again more or less into my normal self, it was nearly time to go on patrol!

As to the activity on the front, it has not been excessive. A fair number of more or less peaceful patrols have gone up, but the weather has been moderately bad. The whole country is under a coating of snow, and some people would no doubt say it looks beautiful. My mind has become so depraved that all I think is, 'By gosh, what a mess there will be when it thaws'. The cold seems to have added considerably to our troubles, because we are having quite an unusual amount of trouble with our engines, mostly carburation. It rather gets on one's nerves at times.

The other day we had a very fine day, so we got up some special stunt, with all three Flights working together. I think the idea roughly was to wipe the Huns from out of the sky. The usual idea! Some engines were however too much for the best of us. For some unknown reason mine declined to function for the first time, and down I had to come into the aerodrome. At one moment all three Flight commanders were on the aerodrome together!

However things didn't go so badly. Three Huns were confirmed, and one or two others felt pretty certain their shots had told. One Hun fell this side of the Lines under control and complete. It was first of all holed in the engine by Herbert in my Flight, when as it came lower archie got another hit on the engine, and after that an RE8 working low had a go, missed, and claimed it! It was finally given to archie to cheer them up. That is what we have to put up with. All our machines returned.

The expert out here now is one McCudden. On the day in question there were eight Huns lying our side of the Lines alone, of which he had three this side. In about three days he brought down eight Huns, seven of which I believe fell this side. An unparalleled success.[6] I suppose he has got about as many as Bishop[7] now; there are several pretty good scores. He is very clever, as of course if a Hun gets this side and sees you, down goes his nose for home again. (The Hun seems to have made up for things somewhat this evening. I have never heard them drop so many bombs.) I am jolly glad I came out on an SE5. They are easily the fastest thing in the sky now, and with a certain amount of patience one can make them fairly manageable. They used to be 150 hp. I have got a 230 hp engine in mine and by taking several inches of dihedral off some unnecessary stability has been got rid of, and better climb and better several other things resulted. The last two days have been completely dud. I don't think I have done much myself. I think I missed another fat two-seater through engine trouble, and did one or two other uneventful jobs.

'The Office' – cockpit dashboard and control column of an SE5A Scout, 1918. Mounted directly in front of the windscreen is the Aldis Sight.

40 Squadron, RFC. 7 January 1918

There has been a good deal of flying weather lately, but there is really nothing of great personal interest to report. Odd pot shots at Huns flying for their lives and sometimes without them is all that happens. The Hun as far as I can see is as usual showing about twice as much common sense as we are. He seems to be resting or re-equipping all his scouts during these winter months and reserving their energy for more lively times. It is very seldom we spot an Albatros scout. Nearly all their work is being done by two-seaters either round about the Lines or very high up. We spend our time wearing out machines which might be more useful in the spring. The other day was beautifully fine and I spent well over an hour with three of my Flight over their Lines, finishing up at all heights, without seeing a thing to go for. Of course, this is a quiet front; there is still quite a rattle going on round Ypres. However, the balance seems to be well on our side at present. The other day you may have noticed we brought down eight this side of the Lines, and about six the other, and only lost one. True, he was a pretty good fellow, with 20 Huns to his credit, but all the same it was a 'bon' day. 40 Squadron contributed materially. I see 40 have brought down about 85 Huns during the year, and three fellows have got over 15 apiece, which is pretty good going.

I have got a pretty stout Flight. Anyway I wouldn't have any other in the squadron as a gift. I impress on them that bringing down Huns is all very well as an amusement, but their first duty after all is to look after me! What is the good of being a Flight commander?! There are seven of us but we usually go up about four at a time (that being the usual number of machines serviceable). Several have been on leave, so four of us have got rather used to one another, and all have done material damage to the wily Hun since I have been here.

Yesterday I had a large number of years chalked off through archie. It was one of his days! I was simply all over the sky; the others said they were kept in a nasty state of perspiration trying to follow me. However, before I left I gave him Hell! I sat about four miles over our side of the Lines and fired both my guns where he ought to have been. The range was not more than eight miles, so I feel pretty certain I got him!!

The best fellow in my Flight is L.A. Herbert. He was a sergeant pilot for some time and has got the Military Medal for bringing down a balloon. He has also several Huns to his credit. A very quiet unassuming fellow, yet one of the best pilots in the squadron. Between you and me I am quite frightened of him! I hope you will meet him one day. He has been out nearly six months, so I am rather frightened I may lose him. There is another fellow called Rusden, who has only been here a short time. I expect great things from him in the future; he is one of my best followers.[8] The others are all the very best, always there if anything is doing, though rather young in their ideas. They are all confoundedly keen, always asking to go up and have a scour round in addition to their jobs.

Our expert, Captain Edward Mannock, has recently been sent home, very much against his will. He has been out here about eight or ten months, and has 18 Huns to his credit. He got his last this side of the Lines the day before he left. He even went up on the morning he was due to leave. I told him to be sure to call on you if he had a chance. He is one of the finest personalities I have ever met. Very popular by all he met, and a regular hero in this squadron. He loved fighting but hated killing – I believe it used to upset him for days after sometimes. He was originally in the ranks and I know you would like him if for no other reason than he is a most arrogant socialist!

He told me he would be staying at the RFC Club, so if he doesn't call on you, you may think it worthwhile to rout him out. He was jolly good to me when I arrived first. A new Flight commander to an old squadron is always looked on with suspicion, and by his being nice to me everyone was. There is another A.1. fellow here called Captain Horsley, MC, an infantry man, who hailed from Oxford before the war. The Garnetts may know his name as he was a rowing man. Wounded three times!

40 Squadron, RFC. 15 January 1918
The only really important difference between this week and previous weeks is that while previously the sun shone, and it snowed and froze, now the sun shines and it rains and thaws. Certainly it is the first time I have been warm, but at the same time I think there is a limit! This blessed spot is about two feet under water, and still going strong. In the cold weather I used to think my hut was very breezy and healthy and that sort of thing. Now I find I would rather have ill-health without the breeze.

The weather has been fairly fine lately and we have flown pretty frequently, but there have been only two or three really 'bon' days.

Albatros D. V Scout, D2004/17 – an example of the most common enemy opponent to be engaged by 40 Squadron in 1917-early 1918.

BELOW LEFT: *The Long and Short of it ... Lt Henry S Wolff standing under the arm of Captain Oswald Horsley, MC, 40 Sqn, Bruay, 1918. 'Shortie' Horsley was tragically killed in a flying accident in England in 1918.* BELOW RIGHT: *LT J W Walwork (left) and Captain C O Rusden, MC of 40 Squadron, who were credited respectively with five and three confirmed victories.*

I'm afraid we haven't been very successful. The Hun has been just a little bit too clever for us, and with the help of his archie signalling has managed to elude us more or less successfully. His scouts are still noticeably absent, but he has a number of two-seaters flying about singly at anything from 20,000 feet to 2,000. The west wind is uniformly blowing, giving the Hun a great advantage. I managed to get in contact with a couple yesterday. One was pointed out by our archies, and was at about 15,000 feet. I was 1500 feet below him. However, he wasn't out to fight and I took up my desired position with ease, and stalled the machine up at him firing both guns, with no apparent success. The range was long and the shooting probably bad, so the Hun was able to make his way. The next moment I spotted a fellow down at about 5,000 so down I went at him, firing with much gusto. This fellow was pretty good, and also evaded me. He was a bit low and diving lower, and also backed up by some very good archies, so I withdrew! Their archie is always on the look-out, pointing out our positions, making it still more difficult. However, we are scheming!

40 Squadron, RFC. 21 January 1918
It hasn't been a very bon day, and I went out with another fellow, and as usual when I can't find much to do, I go and stunt for the infantry, and there I was all over the sky, sometimes under control and sometimes out of control. I threw one loop and jolly near came down into the other man (Usher) which necessitated some pretty rapid calculations! I daresay that is what upset me. We then dived down on our favourite trenches and shot them to bits (I don't think). Anyway both my guns jammed, and I lost my goggles, so it wasn't a bad effort. There is a very hot stuff archie there and I have daily duals with him. He hasn't quite found out the knack of hitting me when I am doing over 150 mph yet! However, he is a spiteful brute.

We have been doing quite a number of jobs lately. Some of them have been on the low side, but others have been anything up to 14,000 feet. Most of our work during the last few months has been taken up with searching out Hun two-seaters and fetching them down. They fly singly and do their best to avoid us; they are sometimes assisted in doing this by very good 'camouflaging' on top. (I apologise for using the word. I suppose you suffer from seeing it in every other line of the Harmsworth press, as much as I do. However, that and 'barrage' are new little words for their pot-bellied editors, and all one can hope for is a speedy end of the war.)

As I have said before, their scouts have been resting, to a large extent, on this part of the Line. They are now appearing in small numbers; not more than 10 have been reported in a bunch yet. I have first-hand evidence of their presence! In case it might amuse you I will run over what happened on the patrol.

I had hoped that five of us would leave the ground together. However, so cunning is this engine of ours that in spite of the fact that five of them were absolutely OK one hour before, only three took it into their heads to be OK when required. Three of us, therefore, departed – the other two left later, I couldn't wait. The two with me were Rusden and Walwork. I made straight for the Lines as I knew a certain Hun artillery machine was working at about 2,000 feet his side of the Lines. While looking round about, I saw some machines very high up well over the enemy's side. We then proceeded to get height, going up and down our side.

At about 11,500 feet I crossed the Lines. The wind, of course, was as usual blowing behind, making us nice still targets for archie on the way home. We passed another small patrol of SE's going the opposite way, which I thought was Tudhope and his lot, but found out later that they had strayed up from another part of the line. Soon after we had passed these lads we crashed into a patrol of five Albatros about 1,000 feet above us. I knew that meant trouble. They had us well their side of the lines, the wind blowing us still further over, the advantage in numbers, and worst of all they were above. After that everybody went round and round, they diving and zooming, while we dodged and tried to stall up after them. Walwork's gun jammed, so he had to pull out. Things looked pretty bright when three more Albatros arrived. However, our luck was in. The other SE's saw us and came to give a hand, and soon after four Camels arrived from nowhere! However, we were all below. We still continued to go round and round and up and down. I learnt my lesson with the Albatros I shot down before. It struck me that they had rather an affection for my streamers, as they seemed to make a special point of diving at me. I expect that is imagination. Everytime one dived from in front, up I went at him, and not being a fool like I was, they pulled off each time. None of them were very keen on close quarters.

This business continued for some time but as Edmund used to say the Huns have a time limit. Rusden and Walwork drove one down,

I saw two Camels push another one down, and I am credited with bagging one out of control, and I sent another one home. When the 'time limit' was up I saw only three above, and they were climbing away. I believe they climb better than we do, though we are a good deal faster. The strange SE's then went south, the Camels to the north, and I finally picked up Rusden again, and we stayed in the middle and patrolled up and down again, our tails more or less up. Of course, it was archie's turn now, and he blazed forth with a good deal of vigour.

Some archies terrify me, others I am frightened of; I respect them all! On some days though I get the better of him. Sometimes if he is shooting well I go slowly, and he lands in front; other times I put up the speed and he bursts behind; other times I climb and he bursts below. When he sees this he bursts them higher and in the meantime I have pushed my nose down, changed direction slightly and increased my speed. This sort of thing happens only *sometimes*. Other days I just shiver, go all out, nose well down and make for home. It is absolutely uncanny the way these fellows bark just alongside of you at say 14,000 feet the very first shot. It takes many seconds to reach you even. Yet artillery machines fly to and fro every day, battery to target, and don't seem to mind if the sky is black with the stuff, and all at about 4,000 feet too. Of course, they get hit about a lot. Well, to continue my story.

Rusden and I continued our patrol to the tune of archie, in a clear sky for nearly another hour. Then three Hun 'Nieuports' turned up. Personally I had had enough and was very annoyed; trembling in every bone, we made towards them, but as luck would have it I had closed my shutters some time before and my engine boiled. That made a fight impossible until it had cooled down, and by that time the Huns had gone. We finished up the show in the usual way. Diving towards the lines in the hope of picking up a two-seater (or not) and finally our little machine gun strafe with archie, or where we think he is, and then into the trenches and home, flying low. So there you have a rough idea of a patrol. Of course, they vary in detail.

The day was good for us. McElroy of A Flight[9] crashed a two-seater Hun in their trenches, and he and Harrison[10] drove another one down out of control. Another squadron drove four down out of control, and another one got crashed and one out of control. That is our front only. The Brigade lost only one machine, so there was some buck in the camp! A Hun out of control is one brought down over the Lines, which is seen by several people, and is considered certain to be done in. You cannot count a Hun crashed unless it is witnessed by ground observers, or else breaks up or flames. Hence the disadvantage of fighting far over the Lines where a scrap is never seen. The whole day was spoilt, as luck would have it, by our general killing himself. The general of our brigade. Shepherd is his name. He was one of the finest fellows who ever lived, with an MC and DSO. Also a topping pilot. He kept a Nieuport for his own use, and I looked after it for him.

While I was up on patrol he had taken it up, and spun into the ground on a neighbouring aerodrome, stunting. He was one of the few fine men at the top of the Flying Corps. There is another in command of training at home. He has already kicked out an incompetent brigadier, a pet aversion of mine, and put a war-timer in his job. Or else Trenchard has done it. Old Shepherd came and congratulated me on my first Hun. Oh! I forgot to tell you the funny part of that little scrap, at least the part that keeps me smiling. I had never considered myself a good pilot, but after that show all hope was bashed to the ground. During that short time I stalled three times, and spun twice, trying to get up at the beggars. Some pilot!

Please tell Ruth I shall write to Mannock and tell him he is not to talk when she wants to dance.

40 Squadron, RFC. 29 January 1918
Things have been livening up a bit lately. The less said about the weather the better. Talk about a winter show. If we have half as many fine days in July I shall simply lie down and die, to save trouble. Most times the mist certainly has the goodness to hang about until about 10 am, but this morning, would you believe it, I was up at 7 am! It really is getting a bit thick! As far as my poor weak memory will support me, I told you about our first mess-up with the Albatri, when I was reputed to have sent one in a headlong hurtling dive to earth! I wish I could have watched it, instead of cracking every bone in my neck, trying to see how far round I could look at my tail. Well, the next day it was worse.

With the usual display three of us got into the air again and started rumbling about. We first of all chased down south after bursts of archie, hoping to find a specimen of the wily Hun this side of the Lines, but no luck. We were only about 6,000 feet. Walwork was with me again, and also Hutton. I looked up over the Hun lines and to my disgust I saw four groups of four and five Huns at heights ranging from 12,000 to 14,000 feet, all running about so as to co-operate with each other. I thought it was a pretty stiff order myself. However, we climbed keeping them well in view, praying that as we climbed we should be joined perhaps by another of our patrols. No luck! I got within about 500 feet of the nearest bunch, and I thought something must be done. So off we struck at right angles and went bang east and right under them.

My whole idea, of course, was to have a short smack at the nearest ones and then withdraw. The usual thing started, the Huns diving from all directions, with much clackity-clackity-clack and tracer bullets flying all over the shop. I dodged the first and then the second came, and round I went under him and shot up. He did some wonderful turn endeavouring to get round behind me again, and started spinning down on top of me. I sort of struck there gaping up, and more or less paralyzed with fright, wondering what the game was.

Finally I realised my manoeuvre hadn't quite suited him, with the result that in his keenness to gain his fifth Iron Cross he had done a dud turn and got into a spin. As he was coming bang on top of me, at last I thought it would be better if I moved on! All this time I had to keep my eye on my two lads and watch the Huns. Already three of these groups had got together, and the fourth had climbed above the mist and was coming up from the south.

My idea was that it was time to sheer off, which we could do, as we were not far from our own Lines. To my horror those two beggars had got right into the thick of things, and were fighting like blazes. Then I saw a Hun dive down, with Hutton on his tail with another Hun behind. He looked as if he was alright, and at last Walwork followed me, and we withdrew when the Huns weren't looking sort of thing. The Huns had the decency to go away at the same time, so it looked quite fair. Our archie said his heart was in his mouth all the time, and there was also some squadron commander up doing a 'shoot' who said that we 'drove the Huns off'!! He reported it to his Wing commander, who was lecturing to all the fighting squadrons in the brigade the next evening, and he mentioned that he had heard that three SE's had driven off umpteen Huns that day, and as long as that sort of thing went on we had little to fear. This colonel only had artillery squadrons in his Wing; we fighting squadrons are in another Wing, and of course exist to protect artillery machines. Well! that was good for B Flight, and owing to my modesty I didn't get up and say that the SE's only ran as fast as they could after a very sharp snap at some silly fat Huns! Since then I have lost my nerve completely – I never go near the Lines under 15,000 feet!

The next day my engine failed me, and Rusden and Hutton went out without me, with orders not to cross the Lines. They attacked a two-seater, and suddenly from nowhere came the usual clackity-clackity-clack; umpteen fat Albatri behind them! Some life! People who don't try have little conception how hard it is to see machines in the air. Poor old B Flight seemed to be out of luck. They seemed to run into the mess every time. At this time the Hun was only doing one job a day when he put up *all* his machines, and left the front more or less clear for the remainder. It's rather a blow if you go up at the same time.

Next day we got off a bit stronger. I was followed by Walwork, Usher (the rag-time king) and Hambley (Canadian, has been on leave for some time). I refused to go near the Lines without 15,000 feet below me, so we toiled all over northern France. Well, we all got there, and I was feeling rather braced, when a light flew out from Usher's machine, and down he went with engine trouble. We were only a short distance over so I let him go. We went on a bit further and could see nothing. Suddenly I saw white archie bursting a long way below and behind me. The Huns usually use black archie and we use white. Down I went very suddenly and hardly noticed by the remainder of my patrol, who had evidently seen Huns, which I hadn't noticed.

Anyway I found a Hun two-seater of a new fighter-type, obviously being archied by his own people as a spoof. Usher was having a go at him on his way down, but he had to clear off. I came down on top of the brute full of gusto, quite certain that I was well backed by the remainder of my patrol, and that the Hun would soon put his nose down and go for home, like all well-behaved Huns. But not a bit of it! There was the little observer crouching over his gun making the usual noises, and the old pilot doing the correct thing, turning as fast as I was, and going just about as quick, too. I thought this is where the science of the game comes in, so there I sat just under his elevator, firing all the guns I could find, and pulling at everything within reach with my usual sang-froid! The Hun, meantime, was leading me a merry sort of dance, and mostly going east.

LEFT: *Lts P D Learoyd (left) and Cecil W Usher ('Pusher') of 40 Squadron, 1918.* RIGHT: *Captains 'Jimmy' Riddle (left), 40 Squadron's Recording Officer (the equivalent of today's sqn adjutant), with George McElroy, MC, DFC.*

Suddenly Clackity-Clackity-Clack and I looked round, and there were three dirty fat white, black and green Albatri diving on my tail. I have never been so frightened in my life. Down I went as fast as I could, and no man has gone faster; engine going like nothing on earth. Luckily we can dive as fast as they can, so they gave it up, fearing something on top of them I expect. I crossed the Lines at a few thousand feet, being archied out of my life. All this didn't take very long, and Hambley soon noticed that I had disappeared, and came down for the two-seater himself, and I am proud to say he destroyed the beastly thing. Nasty greeny brute!

Walwork never saw me go at all, climbed up to 17,000 feet and fought at least three two-seaters up there, so you can see we have got some job. However, my effort to get up to 15,000 feet was wasted. For the next half-hour or so I stuck on the lines, climbing up again. I played sort of hide and seek with one or two more Huns, and as they seemed to increase in numbers, I thought someone else could do a job of work, and I went home. McElroy of A Flight also got a Hun. He gets Huns most days. He specialises in two-seaters and sits up by himself and stalks them. He is a pupil of Mannock's.

The next show I went on I attached myself to A Flight, led by Napier.[11] The usual crowd of Albatri came underneath us this time, together with some two-seaters. There were seven of us up. McElroy went down first after the two-seaters, and others sort of went at various things. I saw a Hun above cunningly trying to get round the back of the show and into the sun. I devoted my attentions to him, and finally lost him in the sun. MacE got his two-seater confirmed as usual.

Another show, we decided to do a show with Camels of McCloughry's squadron. Horsley of C Flight joined me, making five in all. We met the Camels at 15,000 feet. How they got there I don't know. Anyway, they got in front of me as if they were going to conduct the tour, so I took my party right through them and went ahead. They are dreadfully slow up there. There was a thick ground mist coming up from the south, so the Huns wisely did not appear. Also it was in the afternoon and we had the sun well our side. Hambley got detached from me somehow and got lost in the mist and crashed most horribly. No one could have hoped for him to live, but such is the SE5 that all the damage was a broken thumb and very badly bruised in most places. (I forgot to say that the day before when I went along with A Flight, Hutton came too and sent an Albatros down out of control.)

I am awfully sorry to lose Hambley. As you can imagine I am getting to just love my Flight, and it would break my proud heart to drop any of them the other side; at any rate at this time of the year. However, my expert, Herbert, has been on leave. When he comes back I shall be simply terrified! Old Hambley is a very bad Canadian, and if I wasn't out here I should have difficulty in seeing any good in him at all. As a matter of fact, he is one of my best 'comics'. (Usher is my best.) He used to pull the Major's leg and say things to him that a subaltern does *not* say to a CO. He was uncouth, used to bring terrible Canadians into the Mess, and the Major wanted me to get rid of him at one time, but I said I would rather not. Worst of all he drinks too much, wears side-whiskers and sometimes a dirty stock. Really he is a splendid fellow, and I had the utmost confidence in him over the Lines. Best of all, though he used to pull my leg a bit (everyone does), he would do just anything I asked him to, and never worried me in the slightest. Also I could never refrain from bursting with laughter when I spoke to him.

I can tell you I am jolly sorry he has gone. I went to see him in hospital, and I laughed from one end of the time to the other. He had a terrible blotch on his nose, he couldn't shut his mouth, his teeth wouldn't meet, and he got a crick or 'funny feeling' as he called it every way he moved! Another reason for my visit to Hambley in hospital was because I heard that Norman was there. So I routed him out and had a few quiet words with him. The usual bomb raid was in progress in the neighbourhood. He was bombed out of his previous CCS [Casualty Clearing Station].

On the next show I was followed by Walwork, Usher and another lad who doesn't belong to me. I thought we were going to have a peaceful time, but no luck. We wandered up and down over the Lines for some time, when suddenly my black, white and green friends appeared again, about seven in number. We were above and going in opposite directions, so I went straight on, hoping perhaps that they hadn't see us, or else they would think we had seen them. Then round we came with the sun behind. (My strategy is very deep!) Down we went but they were ready. I singled out my sparring companion, but had my calculations absolutely destroyed by suddenly finding he was a new type of two-seater that I knew nothing about.

I pulled away in a hurry. I then had a peck at an Albatros, and I drew away with a gun jammed. While I was getting that right I saw Usher loop and spinning for all he was fit with a couple of Huns above going all out. I got things right and made towards him, but Walwork was there first and they cleared off. So did we! It is strange that that day I felt more than usually scared of the Huns, and felt I would have a game with archie. Yet it is no exaggeration to say that archie has taken many years off my life and I respect him greatly. Well, that day I sat just over the Lines at about 5,000 feet by a very expert archie friend of mine. The great thing about him is that he fires so accurately that one can be pretty certain where his shots will come, always bearing in mind that they take some seconds to arrive. I sat and dodged for 10 minutes to quarter of an hour until the sky was black with the stuff. Every time he got too close I used to dive down and fire my guns at where he ought to be. He got simply furious, and when he was fairly raving I went away.

That same day Horsley with C Flight saw the first Fokker Triplane on this front, and had bad luck in not shooting it down. He drove it down only. Wolff got a Hun.[12] So many lads have been

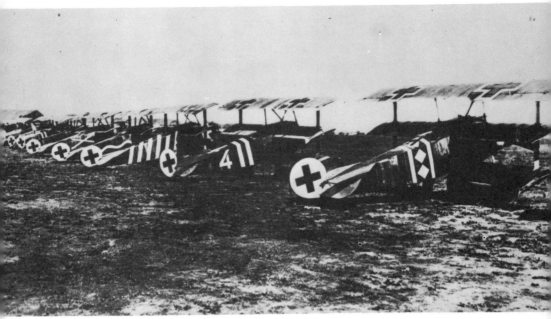

Tripehounds — the Allied nickname for the Fokker Dr.1 Triplane of 1917-18. This view of Jagdstaffel 19, taken in May 1918, shows the variety of individual markings often applied by German pilots — an aid to recognition during combat, apart from personal fancy.

getting Huns lately that really I can't remember who does what. None of ours are missing.

Somebody said he saw six triplanes the other day, so we are looking for some fun.

The working part of my Flight is now in excellent working order. When I first arrived I nearly went off my head. I only just restrained myself from having half of them shot. I have now sacked the Flight Sergeant, and put a junior man in his place. I sometimes shriek at myself the things I say to these men, some of whom are very skilled labour. I told the ex-Flight Sergeant why I was fed up with him and what I thought his shortcomings were. Then I let his successor know what I required of him. These fellows have got just about twice the years and brains of myself. Sometimes I am rather hot stuff and other times I am rotten. I was rather rotten when I let the next senior man know why I had *not* made him Flight Sergeant, but his junior. Oh! it's a funny life!

40 Squadron, RFC. 7 February 1918

I don't know there is an awful lot to write about. Usually we have gone up and chased round clouds, and sort of peeped over the side at archie, and then run back again. One can go quite a long way over the Lines with a feeling of perfect security so long as there is a nice white cloud hiding you from the ground. The Huns on the whole have been fairly quiet. Horsley, with C Flight, let a bunch dive onto the tail of his patrol, but they opened fire too soon. A dogfight ensued, in which Horsley bagged a Hun. Horsley seems to be disappointed they didn't put up a better show. I really don't remember who has brought down Huns. McElroy, as usual, has destroyed several two-seaters. I *do* remember that he brought down two yesterday, and they were particularly scarce that day too. One went down all breaking up, and the other descended in flames, so they were the real thing. The only thing I can remember doing was to chase a fat two-seater for miles with my patrol, and when I caught him up I felt so frightened that I turned round and went back again. We really had got rather far over, and this brute was a gigantic fellow.

Today Tudhope and McElroy have been given MC's, so there is much buck in the camp. They both thoroughly deserve them. Tud has got about seven, and Mac about eight or nine. Tudhope is a hard fighter, and Mac a wily one!

The padres out here make one realise how hopelessly the men at home fail to get at the young men of the nation. All their highly developed theology is all very fine for certain people, but it is only for the benefit of the few who understand it, and doesn't start anywhere near the beginning.

Orchard is the only fellow I know who ever tries to talk so that any ordinary heathen can understand him. Most of these fellows who stand in pulpits I often feel I would like to get hold of, shake them thoroughly, kick them hard, and tell them to go and have a look at the world as it really is, and then start talking about it. No wonder the padres out here feel pretty sick when they are 300 under strength, and no one comes from home. I wonder if it is because they have suffered heavier casualties than any Corps out here! I know the men out here are pretty bad in some ways, but many have jolly fine stuff in them, which only appears out here. What really wants doing is for the Church to be thoroughly washed out, 50 per cent of the padres to be kicked thoroughly and told to wake up, and not to talk nonsense

Padre B W Keymer, the 'spiritual father' of 40 Squadron, 1917-1918, outside his Nissen hut Church of St Michael – titled rather appropriately 'The Flying Warrior', at Bruay airfield. After the war Keymer served at RAF Cranwell, and his suggestion for the new RAF College's motto, Superna Petimus, (*We seek the highest) was officially adopted. He died, of pleurisy, in 1924, leaving seven children, two of whom died in action with the RAF in the 1939-45 war.*

for a living, and then perhaps there will be some chance of we fellows listening to them.

40 Squadron, RFC. 13 February 1918
The weather has been terribly bad lately; in fact it has gradually got worse. I don't mind two days or perhaps three so that we can get straight with our machines, but this sort of business not only gets on one's nerves and makes one unfit, but gives the fat Hun a chance to get on with his work without being continually watched, which is rather serious pour la guerre. That is how such enormous possibilities were opened up for us during the Cambrai show, and also the fact that the only Hun who came over to take photographs and had the necessary information was shot down by archie! Surprise is the only thing that is likely to worry us; otherwise we will simply mop the old boy up if he attacks.

One day during the week I went up to see the 'Great War'. It was not very inspiring as things were rather quiet and we gazed from a distance of about three miles. We had tea in Arras – quite the nicest French town I have been into. Much destroyed by the war of course, the beautiful cathedral being in a most tragic condition. It was a ranging mark for the Huns. It really is tragic to look at the hollow remains. I don't know if the place is so clean because *we* look after it, and not our gallant allies, but it is certainly jolly nearly as clean as a civilised town. I went with Horsley and Jimmy Riddle, our Recording Officer, and we made quite an instructive tour of last April's battlefield. Horsley was in the battle of Arras himself.

Yesterday was quite dud, so Jimmy and I went to meet Tudhope coming from leave. He tells me you had a little party which must have been rather amusing. A good lad is Tuddles.

The old army was very fond of its 'proper channels' for everything. We have excellent remedies for these 'proper channel' experts. We simply ask them to dinner! It is only recently that we have sat on a colonel, torn the leg off a major's slacks, and blacked an adjutant's eyes! Oh it's a 'bonne' spot is La Belle France, though rather dull, as I said for our labour experts.

I am awfully pleased to hear old Mannock has called again. He is some lad! He seems to talk an awful lot of rot though. If he keeps talking nonsense about me ask him how much he wants to borrow next time! And if he must say these things, honestly I wish you would spare me from having to hear it all. Life is quite difficult enough without being told you are the finest fellow that ever lived. I hope you understand what I mean, because I do hate it so, even if it is only meant as a joke.

40 Squadron, RFC. 19 February 1918
Plenty of ground mist, bombing and aviation. We haven't done brilliantly but not too badly. McElroy as usual came to the front, and has now got 12 perfectly good Huns in under two months. Suddenly got his eye in and gone right ahead. Never touched a Hun in his first three months. Now they have taken him away from us and given him a Flight in Edmund's old squadron (24) who are away down south, and are still in the engine trouble period. Rather bad luck on us though, as a lad like that means a lot.

The first day after it cleared up I took my little party up, very glad to have Herbert with me after his leave. He is my 'second', and about

*The author seated in an SE5A of 40 Squadron, 1918. The white 'zig-zag'
marking just visible on the fuselage was a unit marking at that period. The
elongated butt to the upper wing Lewis gun eased handling of the gun on its
Foster mounting.*

40 times as brave as I am. Usher ('Pusher'), Rusden and Horsley
('Shorty') from C Flight were the others. We left the ground
comparatively early, and I returned back fairly chuckling. We
crossed the Lines at over 15,000 feet, struck east, and then made a
drive up the Lines, noses slightly down and plenty of speed, and sun
and wind behind. Lille was just below when I suddenly spotted seven
nasty little things about 1,000 feet above and west. Rusden and
Horsley had fallen out. Round we turned and I sat right plumb
under the back fellow. The funny part was that he didn't know I was
there! I have done a good bit of flying out here, but never have I been
so conscious that I have surprised a Hun. It is a very difficult
performance. The great pity was that he was about 200 yards above
me, which isn't a short range. I just pulled my Lewis gun down and
looked along those dandy little sights that I had put on to satisfy my

vanity more than anything else. Pressed the little trigger actuator, and away spat that dear little specially speeded-up gun of mine. A hundred rounds and he started to turn over, and so did I. I looked over my shoulder, and there was the old Hun going down all over the place. Apparently Usher has had a shot just as I pulled round. Anyway between us we had made him think of home! Old Herbert then came along, followed him down for some way, and seeing he was obviously hit, drew off. The other Huns looking round suddenly and seeing some SE 'Fumfs' and not knowing any better, stuck their noses down, and went like the wind, only a good deal faster. Well, that made me chuckle. May I never be surprised from the west. Just about this time McElroy was driving a two-seater down out of control. Later on we went up again, but the Hun is seldom seen in the afternoon, when the sun is our side of the Lines, and it is very often misty.

Just about the time we were landing there was a stunt effort going on in the bombing line. A certain Hun long-range gun was thought to be knocking too many villages to bits, so they sent about 30 machines to bomb it in the daytime, which of course is a waste of effort on the best occasions. Four RE8's were brought down, and on looking round to find what was wrong we found they were sent up without observers, so as to carry more bombs. I simply couldn't believe my ears when I heard that such things were possible in 1918. It happened on the Somme but I thought those days were over. We were simply furious. It is the biggest victory the Huns have had since I have been out here on this front.

The next day our job was in the afternoon, but we were given a hot air stunt in the morning for one hour. I therefore decided to look after the artillery machines. We were patrolling at about 6,000 feet when away went our archie. Up we went, engines going full out, and found the wicked Hun. Did our best to cut him off, but he was 13,000 and we could only get within 1000 feet. I sat just plumb underneath him with two lads just behind me, looking at his nice little black crosses. Again my gun was brought down, and I fired short burst at him, while the other two pulled up and fired from behind. But no luck, he just sailed gaily on, and went home little troubled but a wee bit frightened. That was bad luck, wasn't it?

We went up the Line again and I thought I would go home. No! I must make sure it was all clear down south again, and then home. Got there and found all the RE8's well our side of the Lines, and hanged if two Pfalz scouts (a new Hun) were sitting on the Lines at about 5,000 feet. They saw us and off they went! Again the good old engine was called for full power, and I was getting well into one at about 130 mph. He had a goodly supply of 'special' ammunition after him at long range, and I pulled off as the Lines were getting left behind, and 11 nasty little specks appeared above.

The next job was to get a new drum on the Lewis gun, always an unpleasant form of amusement. A good fight and I got one on, and the gun pushed into position again. Unfortunately it hadn't clipped, for it came plumb onto my head and bounced overboard! Never been so terrified in my life. My next effort was more successful. Then up came 'Pusher' and pointed heavenwards. No luck! Back we had to go, and there were those nasty specks still there, and to aggravate me still more an RE8 came in front of me and fired a red light. I was just hanged if I was going to go under all this bunch with two others, and one a novice, so I started to climb on my own side of the Lines. So did they! They gradually faded away, so with a sigh of relief I turned for home, having done a 2 hours 15 minutes show instead of one hour. By the time the afternoon show came I was in none too good a temper, but it was misty and I simply climbed up to the Lines, and washed out.

While we had been doing the morning patrol, three of A Flight, McElroy, Wade and Learoyd, had been escorting six DH4's on a bomb raid on some beastly Hun aerodrome. Six Pfalz scouts were waiting for them, and attacked the DH4's. The SE5's then started to spit fire, with the result that Wade shot down two, and McElroy one. All confirmed to have crashed by observers of the DH4's. Another Hun was sent down under control by a DH4. Hit in the engine. This wasn't good enough for McElroy though. After seeing the DH's home, down he goes and crashed a Hun two-seater just on the Lines! Some lad! On the whole I think the Huns went home tails well down.

The next day there was another of these stupid daylight aerodrome bombing stunts, and it was our turn to escort. Herbert, 'Pusher' and 'Rusty' (Rusden) came along, and we met the six DH4's at 15,000 over our aerodrome. Later Rusty had to pull out. The DH4's were well together bar one annoying straggler who required special attention. However we were in great luck, because as soon as we crossed the Lines archie let fly a few rounds, and on looking down there were dozens of little Huns all cracking their neck bones looking up at us, but several thousand feet below. This was very comforting for everyone except any unfortunate whose engine ceased to function. Luckily there were none. These Huns provided a most efficient escort to the objective, which we seemed to take hours to get to. Meanwhile these little fellows were providing an effective screen to archie; they were gradually getting higher and higher and nearer this beastly straggling DH4.

After another half-dozen years had been knocked off my life, the bombers threw off their load, and went hell for leather for home. The Huns kindly turned round with us and helped us back again. As soon as the last DH had crossed the Lines, down I dipped at our 'escort'. Unfortunately my judgement was out of order, and I chose out the leader, a very brightly coloured red fellow. I don't think I got my sights on him even! He went simply all over the sky, and I have never had it slapped so thoroughly across me before. I have enormous respect for that red fellow now!

Meanwhile Herbert had chosen another and got a good bead on him. He thought he got him but was unable to gain confirmation. Pusher must have also got well into a fellow, because he started to spin. I very quickly realised that we were up against no ordinary Huns. They were coloured in every imaginable manner, and my red friend was charging all over the place. Adding to this the fact that we were getting short of petrol, I was rather keen on getting home. Rusden had already run out.

However, this wasn't Herbert's intention. Away he went back again, and started a full-out scrap with a green and white striped fellow. Of course *I* had to go back, and this brought green-and-white's friends back too. I was just getting started with Herb when up came my red friend, with a tartan and one other. I had proper wind-up, but old Herb would go on! The red fellow got into me, and I went down all over the shop, engine well on. Then old Herb took it in the neck and got properly shot up. However he got away whole in body and dropped into an advanced landing ground. These fellows who will fight 11 pugnacious Huns!

Meanwhile McElroy was floating about on his lonelio, and seeing much activity comes along to see what all the row is about. Artful as ever he chooses the most eastern-most one, falls on it by surprise, and shoots it up properly out of control. Some of the other Huns saw that there was an Armstrong Whitworth doing a 'shoot' well below, and thought it would make good fodder. However, this AW

'The Artful Dodger' – two views of the author seated in his SE5A, D3540, 'K' when a Flight commander in 40 Squadron, RAF, 1918. The struts, letter 'K', nose shutters were doped in white and black. The nickname, 'The Artful Dodger', can be seen on the original photo, marked on the lower, centre plate of the nose, in the lower photo. The author claimed four of his twelve victories in this aircraft.

happened to be one who frequently came over to 40 Squadron for practice flights. The first Hun to attack went down in flames, and the second broke into pieces, so that rather spoilt these coloured fellows' game. Unfortunately the red fellow was not one. Anyway, that will stop their laughing in Church!

Since this the weather has been rather misty and less doing. The latest acquisition to the Flight is W.A. Tipton, a Flight commander escaped from the hands of the Turks. A splendid fellow. Hutton has gone sick.

40 Squadron, RFC. 24 March 1918
Well, I had a perfectly priceless leave, thanks to you all. I came back here and didn't know whether to laugh or cry. I expect you saw that the 1st Brigade had brought down 18 Huns in one day. Well, we got 15 in that week, easily heading the list. I got back here on the same night as I left (March 9th). The squadron were at the top of their glory before lunch, and at the bottom after. Seven Huns had been fetched down in the day. In the afternoon Tilney had broken up diving on a Hun, Tipton, who escaped from Turkey, got a bullet in his abdomen and died a few days later, like the hero he was. I never expect again to see a fellow lying halfway between life and death, knowing it, and yet showing such wonderful pluck. Of course he was the real loss.[13] And a fellow called Foster has never been seen or heard of since.[14] While I was on leave Wade was killed, and Herbert wounded.[15] Since then Smith and I had a crash just alongside one another, and his machine burst into flames, and by a miracle he got off with a slightly burnt face.

I arrived back here to find myself in command of the squadron, my Flight, and also Napier's, which was a sort of training show for half a dozen new pilots. From that Sunday to this I seem to have lived in the air. I have got quite automatic about it! I can't remember very much what happens on these patrols. I know I watch the silly altimeter show 17-19,000 feet, get frozen, and then come down again to be filled up. Sometimes we get Huns and sometimes we don't. He doesn't seem very keen on fraternising and mostly gives the cold shoulder. At present the RFC has got its tail well up and the Hun doesn't enjoy life tremendously. However, he makes us think pretty hard sometimes. At night we can't hear each other speak, his engines make such a row!

We have got a new CO from the RNAS – Commander Dallas – a

LEFT: *Captain Richard James Tipton of 40 Squadron, 1918. Born on April 25th 1892, Tipton died of wounds on March 12th, 1918.* RIGHT: *Major Roderic Stanley Dallas, DSO, DSC, commander of 40 Squadron from March 15th to June 1st 1918.*

perfectly priceless fellow. Got 30 Huns himself, but seems to be taking things easy just as present.[16]

40 Squadron, RFC. March 30 1918
There never was such a comic old war as this; it really is quite funny sometimes; usually when it is raining, but even that doesn't stop the comedy these days! We still go on just the same. It would make you roar with laughter! We only had about three machines which would go the other day and we all three sallied forth on a squadron patrol! We are more or less organised again now, but even then all the pilots seem to be new, and what aren't new are on leave, so there you are.

By Jove, I thought I was pretty busy for the first few weeks after leave, crashing up to anything up to 19,000 and coming down so beastly sleepy that there was nothing to do but eat and fall on one's

Pfalz D III Scout – a commonly-met opponent in mid-1918. Of plywood monocoque fuselage construction, the Pfalz displayed many advanced ideas in aircraft design.

bed until the next spasm. However, I have had a bit of an eye opener since then! One day I got sleepy in my machine and I didn't know what the dickens to do. It was with the greatest difficulty that I could keep my eyes open at all, and I didn't know whether to come home or not. However, I woke up before the end all right. Rather a comic life isn't it?

We had been warned ages before that we should have to work down south when the push started, and sure enough it came. It was rather trying at first as we didn't know the country at all well. Before it started all brigades had got the Huns on their front well in hand, and luckily down south they were so nice and tame that they would feed out of your hand! On our front we had been a little excited as the 'Circus' was supposed to be opposite us. However, I don't think they ever functioned. The 'Circus' at present seems to be of about 50 machines. A squadron of Triplanes together with a whole lot of Albatri and Pfalz. I don't think they seem to think the war the best form of amusement though. Old Tud was messing about with a couple of other lads, when he saw about a dozen fat things below, so down he went. No sooner had he started diving than the fat fellows started firing white lights. Tud of course saw that it might be a good game for two or more players but no game for him! He therefore pulled up, looked over his shoulder, and there were hosts of Tripes and things coming full speed ahead out of the sun. Of course he said this is no place for your old uncle, and went straight for home. Well, that's a pretty good 'Circus' for you, isn't it? They are part of the bunch who brought down 93 of our machines since the push started, and of these only five were brought down by their 'star turns'. Some 'star turns' I should think!

When the show started we all thought we had better do something a little special, so we fairly slapped it across him. The Corps brought down 50 or more that day, didn't they? Then the dear old 'Arch-Hun' puts in his 'Official' – 'Our airmen maintained their usual supremacy' and these fat heads started swanking about over their conquered territory. This made us simply furious. I don't think he ended with much swank.

We usually have two squadrons on our aerodrome. The next day there were five! It had been like summer for weeks before this, but this day the clouds came down to a couple of thousand feet. So just to cheer us up they doubled our jobs. We all carried four nice little bombs, and found all sorts of nice funny things to drop them on. At least everything is spoilt at the time by being so frightened, but really there is quite a lot of humour in seeing rows of fat Huns walking along a long straight road, laying nice little eggs on them, and then shooting them up with a couple of guns, and seeing them run in all directions, and pretty fast too.

Its funny enough when one sits in a nice comfortable hut, but it doesn't seem funny when the clouds are at 2,000, when the air is swarming with your own machines, and you feel frightened to move, when archie starts pitching them all over you, and machine guns crack from below. The only thing that didn't add to the humour of the show was the Hun Flying Corps; that seemed to be resting! The first day of this low stuff archie had got left rather behind; on the second day he was well up, and a few Huns were seen by reckless people who went too far over. The poor old Hun was so upset that he refused to walk along his roads, and used to take to open country.

We sometimes concentrate on one bit of the line and sometimes on another. Last time I found a couple of Hun batteries much too busy, so I laid on them and shot them up a bit. I didn't see the firing again, so perhaps they found some dugouts. The poor old 'kite' was rather shot up though, so I have just got a new one. We have done our best to cheer up the infantry. This is probably the first time he has really seen the Corps since the war started. Before we have always been too high. Our infantry gets wind up when one Hun shoots a few rounds over their heads, so I bet the Huns have had a little 'wind' all right. The troops on the ground have fought simply magnificently. I should think Herbert Gough's Army has made rather a mess of things on the first two days, but Byng must have got a lot of credit for his part. His lot have withdrawn mostly to conform with the line, fighting every foot, and inflicting terrible losses, which is obvious by the way the Hun has been pushing in his divisions. The whole show is against tremendous odds, and is an absolute death or victory push for the Huns. There are wonderful stories of how these infantry fellows are fighting. However, we haven't finished yet!

Yesterday towards dark it started raining heavily, so six machines were ordered up. Funnily enough they all came back, and our general was so annoyed at their safe return that he sent a hearty congratulation on the splendid performance! In fact I don't think the army in general has ever been congratulated quite so much since they began to run. Gives these Parliament blokes something to do I suppose. As soon as they see their necks are more or less safe again, off they will start. I suppose their first effort will be to kick out Lloyd George and D – Haig! Something to do I suppose!

Did you read that stuff by Prince Funny-face, who was German Ambassador in London before the war? The best thing I have read for a long time. Do you think it would be a good thing if I took a permanent job in the Royal Air Force if they give me a Flight? I don't seem to be cut out for anything very special do I? Pretty comic job, but I don't know of any better.

40 Squadron, RAF. 8 April 1918
Our new CO, Dallas, is a splendid lad. Tall, good-looking, a wonderful specimen of manhood, very reserved and charming; a veritable flapper's idol! He hasn't flown much with us yet, but I think he will when he gets straightened out. He has a great score of Huns, varying from 30-37. He was considered the star turn of the RNAS and the practical expert adviser. So we were pretty lucky to get him. I only wish he had come a few months earlier, when the squadron was more settled, and the 'new' element was not quite so strong.

My Flight has changed considerably, but though it is not quite so strong as it used to be, it is shaping itself into a very fine style. Once

40 Sqn pilots and ground officers, Bruay, April 1918. From left: Capt W L Harrison, MC; G A B Wheldon (Equipment officer); Unknown; H S Cameron; C W Usher; J W Walwork; J H Tudhope; Author; Major R S Dallas, DSO, DSC; Padre B W Keymer; and Lt L H Sutton.

or twice I have had hasty words with certain new members, as to their ideas of formation flying. They have taken effect and we now are shaping toppingly in the air again. We used to pride ourselves on our formation. Really I have nothing to be anything but very proud of. Walwork (my 'second'), Usher and Rusden form a very fine fighting head. All have done very good work and take a lot of beating. Then come three new lads – Hind, Captain Middleton and Murman. Middleton will be very stout, Hind is good but lacks individuality for the time being; Murman is disappointing. Tud's Flight is much better than it used to be, and together work toppingly. He is a braver man than I am, so I always get him to lead and I usually fly above him.

We haven't been doing any very special low strafing lately, which is rather a relief. Tud and I made rather a mess of a show the other morning by flying just alongside a bunch of Huns without recognising them. We then got amongst about 27 of them after having lost certain advantages, and only got one or two. They rather messed up our little plans by getting above and below us. However, they were very weak-kneed, and might easily have afforded excellent targets for the young and enthusiastic aviator.

They delayed my return home, and nearly caused my ruin. I was contour-chasing home with my patrol; had just passed over a favourite CCS, and was about three feet off the ground ready to zoom a light railway embankment, when my engine cut dead out through lack of petrol. I made some swift calculations badly, touched the ground with my wingtip, with the disastrous result that I turned some four or five somersaults on the ground, ending up head down, with the tail alongside the engine, and the Lewis gun prattling merrily.

I undid my belt, crawled out, still smiling, to gaze upon my first RFC crash!

Stretcher bearers then hurried upon the scene from the favourite CCS, which is reputed to habitate a 'lovely' with golden locks, and loth as I was to refuse, I declined their kind offer, stopped a colonel in a car, and got back here! For punishment I had to fly someone else's kite on the evening job – a thing I detest doing. However, it wasn't the first time.

40 Squadron, RAF. 14 April 1918
As far as an unbiased spectator can judge, the War still continues – at least, this is the conclusion I have come to from fairly diligent reading of the *Daily Mail*. Apparently we are still 'winning', so it doesn't look as if the summing up is very near at hand. We have lost all the guns and most of the men on the front, but as this was fortunately anticipated by Sir Henry Wilson and Lloyd George, we have little to worry about in this respect. I don't think I told you that we had two MC's in the squadron for the low strafing we did down south. Horsley was one, and as he had an MC in the infantry, he has now a Bar. This, of course, was the most popular move possible, as there is no finer fellow in the squadron. What is more he doesn't go out to win decorations, but simply does his job to the best of his ability. The other MC went to one W.E. Warden.

Everything was going famously a short time ago. The war was being slowly lost down south, but we had given up watching the show, so what did we care? We looked after our own little show which was really quite a respectable little affair. Then suddenly everything was spoilt; the blank German started disturbing the peace north of the canal! In no way could they have annoyed us more. We couldn't have the Huns playing any silly little monkey tricks on our little patch. Unfortunately the day commenced with a thick fog. It was almost impossible to see across our tennis court, and all we knew was that the Portuguese Army were all in a sort of marathon competition; no one knew much except that the Huns were being nasty. Towards the close of the evening a few of us managed to get up with four little bombs. It was absolutely filthy, but I could just clamber through the mist and spread a few eggs in the neighbourhood of La Bassée, and shoot a few rounds at odds and ends. The next day was worse than ever. Down south the roof was at 2,000 feet which was nearly ideal, now we had thick mist at 800 feet and no visibility. I managed to stagger about, drop the pills, with usual lack of accuracy, and shoot about with mg's. Drove a Hun away, and then got driven by five. That was almost a pleasure!

Since the Huns attacked down south they have learnt a thing or two. They saw this machine gunning was quite good sport for two or more players, and now they have nests of those beastly machine guns waiting for us, and they simply wipe years off one's life at a flash! At the end of the first day or so, we left Bion missing, and Carnegie wounded but OK. Bion heard his brother was killed two or three days before. Rusden was flying about at about two feet, when he heard 'Clackity-Clackity-Clack', looked round and saw a fat Hun two-seater. Turned round and shot it down, and had the pleasure of seeing it crash good and hearty into the ground. Tudhope also sent an Albatros spinning into a cloud.

In the afternoon it cleared up somewhat, much to everyone's absolute delight, so much have our ideas on weather conditions changed. No sooner crossed the Lines than along came about eight Triplanes. Tud immediately sent one crashing to earth. I had a bang but was let down by guns. However, I found one of these stupid little things by itself a few moments later and shot it down, confirmed by archie. The mist returned later. Before the close of the day 'The Admiral' (CO) had gone up by himself, and to his surprise was shot at from below. Looked down, saw a fat Hun two-seater, which he promptly shot down and crashed. On his way back potted at a balloon. He is the most wonderful fellow that ever lived!

The next day was the most wonderful day I have ever seen in France, and as usual just ideal for the Hun sur terre. It gave him a chance to find himself and collect his bits together. I could see England as clear as anything, and several times I thought of letting my foot slip on the rudder! In the early morning Napier had his Flight up and I lent him Hind. Most of them were new pilots so the 'Admiral' went up too. They got into about a dozen Huns, and Hind pushed one down. Five of these Huns on being attacked played their usual trick of climbing. Dallas therefore climbed alongside them just out of range, and so kept them from diving down. This probably saved a couple of young pilots!

In the afternoon show I took my Flight up. Two of them old and two new hands. We first cleared a couple of two-seaters off at the double. Some Camels may have got one; my guns let me down. Saw specks in the distance, so climbed quick into the sun. Turned round and were above eight Hun scouts. Had a perfectly splendid scrap for about 20 minutes, full of humour. I must have dived onto them six or eight times, and every time I pulled up I had to pump pressure to keep the engine going. They were quite good and chased each other's tails whenever attacked, and did their best to plonk a few shots in on the upward journey. We started at 12,000 and left four of them all out for home at 5,000. Walwork, Usher, Middleton and self all put one down out of control. In the evening the 'Admiral' again went up, with Horsley ('Shorty'). They attacked seven Huns, and Shorty shot at one which he forced to land. The others ran away, except one which went down to about 5,000 and watched his friend land. The 'Admiral' dropped down and crashed him into a hedge a few fields from his friend. Some lad, isn't he?

So here we are working like nothing on earth, and instead of praying for dud weather, we pray for a blue sky! What a war! I had better luck with my bombs a day or two ago. In the morning the mist improved somewhat. I went out to bomb canal bridges. Funnily enough I found some, dropped the eggs, saw one burst. It was a miss but not too bad for me. I was in too much of a hurry to get away to see the others! I then buzzed round to another canal and used my mg's with some vim on a couple of other bridges, and on a near town. Later in the day I went to destroy and reconnoitre a big road. I got well along over a village and pulled the plug. Looked back and to my amazement I had hit two houses closely lining the road, and both were burning in a most wonderful manner. You would have shrieked with laughter to see those fat little Huns below running everywhere, with a warm seat to their trousers! Absolute luck, of course, but adds humour to one's job.

Today was worse than ever. Mist very low, but visibility better.

The army were all at sea (not unusual) and very much wanted a reconnaissance of certain parts. A matter of distinguishing uniforms. Napier, Horsley and I said, 'Right-O'. At the last moment the 'Admiral' says he is coming. We do the job and satisfy the army. The 'Admiral' goes mad and gets wounded in the knee (flesh) and ankle. Horsley got a bullet just behind his backside. The stupid 'old thing' thought it was the best joke that had ever happened, and after a lot of trouble we have bundled him off to hospital. Our great trouble is to get him back again, which I think we shall succeed in doing as his wounds are slight.

We haven't moved our aerodrome yet, though the Huns have advanced north-west of it. We are not anxious to do so, as we never get bombed here. The conclusion is that there are too many good spies about!

40 Squadron, RAF. 24 April 1918
Our work lately has been very disappointing. We have been going at a very steady high pressure, and mostly in pretty beastly weather. Horsley (Shorty) and I have been working mostly together, and have put a considerable amount of vim into our shows with very little success. Time and again we have worn ourselves out without seeing a single Hun, and at other times we have seen them without being able to catch them. We had possibilities of a good show the other day when I made a mess of it. We had been patrolling for a long time without seeing anything, and I had just pulled back my throttle to glide home when I saw four fat hairy-legged Pfalz scouts below. We were only about a mile over.

I increased the angle of descent and was just getting a lovely bead into what seemed like pretty good meat, when I happened to lift my eyes a little and there were eight stupid little Tripehounds diving on us with considerable zeal. I had but one thought! Up I pulled, round and down the other side, and home as fast as possible. My patrol followed à la text book, and we did a most masterly wheel and dive out of danger's way. We never play about with Tripes, when they are above, and keep away from close quarters whenever possible. They can manoeuvre much better than we can, but have not nearly so much speed. I can tell you I chuckled a bit on that rush down-hill for home!

In the afternoon Salmond[17] came round, and as I was senior Flight commander about, he asked to see me. We were getting quite

*Relaxing outside the squadron office in May 1918 are (from left) Cecil Usher;
Major Roderick Dallas; Captain Ian P R Napier, MC and Captain C O
Rusden, MC.*

friendly when he said, 'Well, Lewis, been getting many Huns lately?'
– 'No, sir, but we got chased out of the sky a couple of hours ago'.
Rather amused the old boy, I believe.

I was just dying to ask him why Trenchard had left, but didn't
quite dare. It has made everyone out here absolutely livid, of course.
Nothing has upset my confidence in the Lloyd George newspaper
show so much. I didn't care a hang about Robertson going, and
didn't take much interest when Jellicoe was given his ticket, but here
is a fellow I know. One who I disliked before I knew him, and
admired when I did. I believe Trenchard is an exceptional man, let
alone the fact that he has built up the RFC in France. There is none
of the regular soldier touch about him. He doesn't smoke, and I have
never seen him drink anything but water, and one stares at a *general*
who lives like that. I think he was generally regarded by the RFC
and the RNAS as the 'big noise' of our show, and of course he is very
strong-minded and independent. At the same time he has the
experience, and our present position out here now is largely the
result of his efforts. He would have frightened the lives out of those
whiney men in the Hotel Cecil. I believe all the people in the Cecil
sent in their resignations, but were not accepted. We have thought of
sending in all ours, but then they would refuse to accept them, and

then the only thing that we could do would be to refuse to fly, and of course the progress of the war would suffer. But really it is the worst bit of jobbery one has ever come across. As for Sykes,[18] it more or less goes without saying that he is no use to us.

Our old 'Admiral' has got out of hospital and has been lying up with the squadron. He is getting on fine, and today has been able to hobble on a couple of sticks.

We have now got a new form of amusement. We spend most of our nights trembling in every nerve while high velocity shells pitch within a few hundred yards of us. Most of them pitch in a little valley just the other end of the aerodrome, but at other times they drop them around the town. They make an enormous noise and cause great damage. The losses amongst the civilians have been very heavy but numbers of them have left now.

Old Tudhope left us the other day. He is a great loss, but it was full time he went home. He nearly fainted in the air. He was an extraordinary example of doing every job thoroughly and without any pot-hunting. His Bar has come through to his MC and no man deserved one more. I saw him off to Boulogne – the first time I have dared to leave the squadron for more than five minutes for weeks. Mannock came across again the other day. He has got two or three more Huns.

We are all quite bucked that Richthofen is under the soil. Shot down by a Camel while attacking an RE8. Never admired him very much as he was such a boaster. I don't think the Huns were very fond of him either.[19]

40 Squadron, RAF. 24 May 1918
I had a lovely leave, it seems like months ago, though they tell me it is only in the region of a week. Things had been going very well in the squadron while I was away. Napier had got several Huns and the MC. He has at any rate deserved it, as he really has done some good work. The 'Admiral' has started flying, and is quite mad. He went over to Douai aerodrome and dropped a pair of boots with a message to the effect that as the Huns couldn't come up and fight he was afraid they must be wearing their boots out. One unfortunate Hun 'got in my way' on the return so he shot it down and saw it crash! When the men went to gather up the boots he dropped a couple of bombs on them! Since I have returned he has one day shot a balloon down, failing to find anything better; another day he followed a very

high Hun for an hour and a half without being able to climb up to it, until it was over Lille. The Hun then put its nose down to descend, whereupon Dallas sent it down in flames.

Another day he did a similar show but the Hun knew he was there, and wouldn't come down, so he saw a large formation of Hun scouts below. He flew alongside the back man until he had seen all he wanted to of him, and then shot him down hopelessly out of control. This woke up the rest of the formation, who immediately went spinning down, one and all! I think he has got one other, and added to this he has had one or two cases of bad luck through gun trouble. I think he has got 37 Huns now.

One lad was lost while I was away on leave, by name of Andrews. Shewed great promise but had only been with us a short time.[20] Since then we have lost two youngsters of the very best. One by name Seymour was in Shorty's Flight and was a perfect topper. Very, very keen and doing very well, and more was expected. I'm afraid I must have been somewhere near when he was done in, though I didn't see it. I happened to be roving by myself at the time, when I saw an SE fire a red light. I followed and soon spotted eight Huns fairly well over. To attack eight Huns alone one must have considerable experience and many advantages, of which height and surprise are perhaps the most useful. I lost sight of this lad on approaching these fellows as he was below me, and I was a good deal taken up in deciding how and where I was going to attack.

As soon as I dived down the Huns all split up and started flying all over the sky. I very much fear this lad must have been carried away by over-enthusiasm and got in amongst them. I could find no trace whatever, and was very, very sorry to find it was he when I landed. He was a most promising fellow and Shorty thought no end of him.[21] I later on found a low two-seater and was just going to have a crack at him when crowds of machines started diving on me out of the sun. They may have been ours for all I know! I didn't wait to see! Too much confidence is a very bad thing.

The spirit of this squadron is simply wonderful now. All due to the 'Admiral', or the 'Old Fool' as we sometimes call him. Everyone adores him and everyone is full out to bring down Huns as a result. Unfortunately we have had some very bad luck and have an everlasting fight with our engines. However, it is awfully topping having such a fine atmosphere, especially when one visits some other squadrons. A great thing I think is that there is practically nothing

Major Dallas seated in SE5A, D3511 — an aircraft flown on occasion by the author, and George McElroy. The partial 'camouflage' here was probably for some specific low-level operation(s). This photo was actually taken on May 28th 1918 — only three days before Dallas was killed in action.

drunk but soft drinks, so that the Mess is always full of spirit without any artificial stimulants. My Flight has got into full swing again and is as good as ever. I just love having them around me. My doubtful pilot got a Hun down out of control while I was on leave, after a talk with the CO, which has made me very pleased. I always like having everyone in the Flight with a Hun to his credit. They have all been bringing them down lately, 'Pusher' (Usher), Rusden, Hind, Middleton, 'Bolo' and Murman.

Tragic to relate Shorty has cracked up and Rusden has been given C Flight. I am very pleased, of course, as he deserves everything he gets. He is a splendid fellow, but at the same time I lose him. Also, as Napier is on leave, I have lent Pusher to run A Flight, so we seem to be running most of the squadron. In exchange for Rusden I have got a new pilot, a hefty great Yank, an awfully good fellow I should think. We have also got a Yank major attached to us as a flying officer. I rather want to see him leave the formation or something, so that I can tell him off. Rather good fun ticking off majors! As Napier is on leave I have been leading all the squadron shows lately.

Old Shorty (Horsley) always used to fly on my right, and he would stick right close there as if tied to me; it was priceless. It didn't matter a hang what the other people were doing, he was always there. We had one great show together when we dived on a two-seater out of the sun and surprised him. He went below and I dived on top and we missed the brute. Shorty's gun jammed when he was very nearly hitting the fellow, and he was using some very bad language when he returned. Two or three days ago the poor old fellow went all wrong in the air. His legs became sort of paralysed and his hands swelled up to a tremendous size. He was really very lucky to have got down – a horrible experience. Even then he followed just behind until nearly the end of the patrol. I last saw him at a base hospital, quite recovered, but he is sure to be sent home. He was miles and away the finest fellow in the squadron, and the 'Admiral' was quite devoted to him. I really don't know how we shall get on without him; I don't know how I shall.

It was on this last show that we lost a little fellow called Watson. An awfully stout little lad, who had shot a Hun down in flames over Lille only the day before.

I dived down towards our Lines towards the end of a patrol and several fellows thought they would stick around and see if they couldn't pick an odd Hun or a balloon up before the conclusion. They therefore very annoyingly split up a bit. Several unseen Huns then came bounding down on us, and the first thing I knew was young Hind diving like the dickens with three Huns behind him, and just passed close to me. That didn't seem right so I turned round, and had a very deuce of a scrap with these three lads. They kept diving on me in turn, and I had to turn and dodge each fellow and watch the bullets stream over my head. Two of them soon got tired and went, and I then got below the tail of the third and shot for all I was fit. He seemed a pretty rotten pilot, but I was evidently a worse shot, because nothing seemed to worry him at all, so I let him go, feeling very upset. I am afraid some other ones must have got into Watson, because he was reported as having gone down out of control. I suppose he can't have seen them, which was a great pity.[22]

The next day we had another quite good fight before breakfast. I was leading about nine machines when I saw a bunch of what looked like Huns on about the same level and about the same in number.

Major Keith ('Grid') Caldwell, MC, DFC, the distinguished New Zealand 'ace', then commanding 74 Squadron, with the author's father, during a visit by Caldwell in 1918.

Luckily I decided to work round behind them because a second crowd soon came into sight. We therefore worked round behind these fellows who were slightly below. I got into one of the back ones and shot him up properly. He turned over on his back just as I was nearly hitting him, and went down toppingly, falling all ways. The others then came back, making about 20 against us. We dived and shot at them for a long time, and finally left them pretty low over Douai.

I had a bang at a two-seater very low down, diving at the front of him on the way back. He completely put me off by firing over his top plane from the back seat, so I left him alone, like the determined fighter I am. When we got back I found Wolff had seen my Hun go down, and had been equally impressed as to the hopelessness of the poor fellow over flying at the back of his formation again. However, as we were engaged in a pretty big dogfight at about 16,000 feet, no one had been able to see him crash; and it was too far over for the ground observers to see the show at all, so as per usual I am credited with another Hun out of control, which isn't worth a cuss.

The weather has been terrific, and the heat stifling. We have found a pretty priceless pond to bathe in! It looks like a large crater. Anyway, it is about 450 to 300 yards, and the banks go straight down. It is said to be about 200 feet deep, so with the help of rafts, planks, a canoe, a football, and a few elementary swimming strokes, we have the very best of fun.

You will be delighted to hear that Mannock has been awarded the DSO. I rang him up to congratulate him and he told me he has now got 41 Huns, so he is probably at the head of the list of people at present out here. His fighting partner has been shot down after bringing nine down.

* * *

LETTER FROM CAPTAIN OSWALD HORSLEY (40 Squadron)

Saville Club
107, Piccadilly, W.1.
6 June 1918

Dear Mrs Lewis,

Many thanks for your very kind letter. I should like to come and see you very much. I am afraid though that my tennis is a disgrace to

The author's mother.

the RAF and that my horticultural experience has hitherto run to nothing more ambitious than mustard and cress on damp flannel, but the flesh and spirit are both willing for encouragement in either of the above acts.

I am enjoying five weeks' leave at the present moment and the medical authorites can find nothing wrong with me, and as far as I can see from the point of view of an invalid I am a complete fraud.

I hope Gwilym will soon be home again for a turn of Home Establishment – no one deserves it more than he does. I hope he will be able to drag himself away from 40 where he is, of course, the leading light. The very day I left the squadron he had crashed another Hun, and only a short while ago I heard of yet another – this time in flames.

I feel extremely guilty being at home in these days, especially when the leeches insist that I am perfectly well, which verdict coincides exactly with my own feelings.

Yours sincerely,
OSWALD HORSLEY

*   *   *

40 Squadron, RAF. 6 June 1918
The world is upside down. I don't know where to start. In the first place Dallas has been killed; I can't think why, but he has been. Too good for this world, I suppose. As was his custom, he went out on his own to strafe high reconnaissance machines. He must have been coming back when he saw a Triplane just our side of the Lines. Of course, it had to be destroyed, and in the meantime two other Triplanes descended from a great height, and shot the poor fellow through the head. He fell this side of the Lines, with a very sound 40 Huns to his credit. He never claimed anything he wasn't absolutely certain of.

We simply couldn't believe our ears when we first got the news, but all the same it was true. It wasn't a matter of admiring the 'old fool'; we simply adored him. He must have had a most wonderful influence because the squadron has had awfully bad luck, and a very large element of new pilots. Yet the spirit has been wonderful. There never was such a happy bunch of lads. I feel I have lost a very good friend as well as a CO. Since I returned from leave we got to know each other awfully well, and had all sorts of discussions on the

Roderic Dallas's grave in the British cemetery at Pernes, France, 1918.

squadron and pilots in it. He had got everyone summed up properly, and knew everything worth knowing about the lads. He seldom, if ever, said or seemed to think anything but nice things about everybody.

The worst of the whole thing was that he had almost fixed up to take charge of all testing in England, and we all saw possibilities of a sort of reunion in England under him. He would have been largely responsible for the selection of new machines. However, that is no more, and we no longer have our 'Admiral'.[23]

We have again been very lucky in our new CO. Major A.W. Keen, MC is his name and just before I arrived here he had Tudhope's Flight in this squadron. He is a fine Hun strafer, and though a younger type of squadron commander, is possessed of a very striking and independent personality. To help us in what seems to be a new start, we have moved our aerodrome [to Bryas]. We are in the same neighbourhood but further back. Since my return from leave the Hun has been pushing his bangers, both day and night. Twelve and 15-inch shells have been constantly crashing in the proximity of the aerodrome, and added to this the everlasting nocturnal aircraft visits with their accompanying AA and machine gun fire, several of the fellows haven't been getting sufficient rest.

The Huns' night bombing raids are quite a source of amusement. The searchlights are very good round us, and we have an MG placed just near the Mess, so as soon as we hear an engine a rush is made for the gun. If the searchlights pick out the Hun, no matter whether he is 2,000 or 20,000 feet, we fire! Archie brought one down in flames quite near the other night. Quite a good sight.

A few nights ago we managed to find a few (Huns), about eight. We were about the same in number. I got onto the tail of one stupid lad who didn't seem to quite know what to do. I gave him a good deluge with both guns and he went down in flames. Hind picked up another, which we all saw crash as it burst into flames as soon as it hit the ground. The 'Admiral' cut across from another quarter of the heavens, swearing he was not going to miss the show, and crashed one lad, and sent another out of control. A Bristol Fighter then got another, so I don't think those fellows had a very enjoyable patrol.

Mannock came here a few days ago. He has now got a Bar to his DSO and by bringing down three the night before has now 51 Huns to his credit. James McCudden was the leader on the British side before with 52, so you see you know someone pretty important!

40 Squadron, RAF. 17 June 1918

Life has been extremely dull lately. The attack down south has robbed us all of the chances of doing what we are, I suppose put here to do. Time after time, day after day, I have patrolled the whole sky at all heights in all places, and found nothing, or perhaps seen a couple of Huns playing at hedge-hopping about five miles over their Lines. Such a life becomes very enervating, even for an old 'home bird' like myself, as it is difficult to keep one's efficiency without some little success now and again. However, I very much suspect that we are due for a bigger visitation soon, and I guess we shall have to keep the eyes skinned a bit then. No Triplanes on my tail without permission, I hope! However, even a Tripe is not much good without a man inside it!

I had been in the habit of going up with another lad or two, to see if we could smack a Hun, as the sun was setting. We would very often join another of our patrols if we could find one. As often as not I would take 'Bolo' (Poler).[24] Usher is my 'second' now, and very good as a leader too, but a trifle independent for what I wanted. Hind will, I think, do *very* well later, and he often used to come with me. He, however, likes to review a situation before he attacks, though when he does, he does! A very useful member of the formation, especially as he ticks me off. He gave me quite a dressing down the other day for pulling out from an attack when my guns jammed. He told me I must carry on, or else the lads behind will think I am abandoning the fight, and that they must do likewise. And by jove, he is right! He is on leave just now, and though it's his first he has got several Huns!

Captain Middleton is now back from leave and is becoming quite a humourist. He is just now in the front row with 'Pusher'. What old Dallas used to call the 'fighting head'. Then there is a very hefty Yank called Burwell who hasn't got a Hun yet, through lack of opportunity, although I don't think it will be long before he does. The other member of my Flight, Murman, I have become quite reconciled to, though I didn't like him at first. The 'Admiral' must have had a wonderful influence over him, because he goes into a scrap now shooting right and left, never looking behind, and comes out with his machine shot all over the shop. We call him 'The Baron', and he is now considered one of B Flight's comics!

Rusden's heart went all wonky so he went home, and we are all delighted to have McElroy back again in his place. He had 25 Huns before he went home a month or two ago.

Three Americans who served in the author's Flight – Don S ('Bolo') Poler; Paul V Burwell and Major R M Davis.

40 Squadron, RAF. 28 June 1918

We have put in quite a heap of work, which up to a point does everyone a lot of good. Further than that I have actually seen some Huns, which is quite an event. I expect you saw that Wüsthoff was brought down this side of the Lines. No 24 Squadron got him down, and I believe he was awful sick because his patrol left him.[25]

The other day we chased a two-seater down, and I had to give it up as my guns gave trouble. Rather sickening as we had got the old fellow in a proper dive, and the observer behind can't shoot when the dive is over a certain speed. Two very sporty Hun scouts attacked a straggler of our formation. One with a very bright red top plane and yellow body, and the other a mottled brown. I turned round on them and had a shot at the brown lad, but this time had trouble with the engine.

Bolo had an excellent fight with the red fellow, who fought with equal determination, finally leaving each other at a few thousand feet. The brown lad, who was flying a machine I didn't know, but shall next time, also put up a very good show. His machine was probably a Fokker biplane which really is quite good stuff, and is flown now by the Huns who fancy themselves most. Middleton pitched into him, and got his machine badly shot about, and also his lateral control, and finally Murman chased him well over towards Douai. As we failed to get either of them, I can't help thinking that they won. However, they are the best two Huns I have seen for many a long day.

I have a great deal of fun with my Flight now. Our formation flying is our great point; no matter what way I turn they are always there, and now several of them 'roll' as we go along, which makes me roar with laughter. To 'roll' you turn over on your back, and continue turning over until you come the right way up again. Old 'Pusher' used to be the great expert at that. He used to perform over the trenches too, and then fire into the Hun front line. Unfortunately we said goodbye to him the other day, after an eight or nine months sojourn in this land. Hind has just returned from leave, and will take his place as my deputy. In Pusher's place I am very lucky in getting a fellow called Trubshawe, whom we applied for. He is Shorty's greatest pal, and just full of pep. He is just like a thin version of Shorty, but hasn't got the humour. However, he is one of the very best. Always worrying me to take him up with the patrol!

I don't know if I told you, but we have McElroy back with us again. He is a wild youngster, went home and refused to instruct, and quarrelled with most people, and soon applied to come overseas again. Before he went home he had got 30 Huns and also a balloon.

40 Squadron, RAF. 11 July 1918
Things have livened up considerably lately; the Hun seems to have come back to see us in a greater or lesser degree, with the result that the '40th Pursuit Flight' has had to make their welcome as cordial as possible. Nevertheless the Hun does not seem quite so tame as he used to be. He has got a new machine called the Fokker biplane, which requires quite a lot of careful study now and then, and also he has got a more powerful engine so that the stupid fellow goes as high as he likes, and that spoils a heap of fun because if he goes right up there we can't dive on him.[26] Worst of all, the dear Pfalz, on which I was going to make my reputation, he mixes up with Triplanes, and so one has to be ready for all sorts of tricks!

The other day I had rather an amusing patrol. We (my Flight) joined in the tail end of a scrap in which A Flight was concerned. I managed to frighten a couple of biplanes off Clarke's tail, and saw him across the Lines, but unfortunately they had hit him in such a way that he won't be able to sit down comfortably for some time.[27] Middleton got his machine badly shot about, through over-enthusiasm after a Hun. Just as this little show was terminating, and the Huns had been driven down very low on their side of the Lines, I saw a higher bunch come up, about our own in number. For about 35 minutes I tried to get at these fellows, Pfalz and Triplanes: seeing they could climb as fast as I could I gave up trying, and waited for them to come down on us. We were right over their side, and I flew alongside and below, but nothing doing.

Finally I got so fed up that I started throwing my machine all over the place, and the others stunted as hard as they could. I think this must have absolutely put the lid on the Huns and frightened them to death. But they still hung up there, so I dived right under them, and then away so that they could get on our tails. The leaders must have puffed out his chest a bit then, and thought of all the Iron Crosses he had won, because he started to dive down on the back man, and fired some of his beastly tracers at us from about a mile. Up I pulled again, thinking the show was going to start, but No! This gallant lad pulled up and went straight east! They are not all quite as bad as that!

Captain George Edward Henry McElroy, MC, DFC, the leading Irish fighter pilot of 1914-18. Seen here with an SE5A which carries four 25lb Cooper bombs under its fuselage.

Fokker D.VII – one of the finest combat aircraft used by the Germans in 1918.

McElroy has been going absolutely full-out. He is quite mad and seldom returns without having brought something down. If he can't find a Hun he shoots a balloon, and gets all the machine guns on the front onto him. He has now got 37 Huns and three balloons! He never troubles to climb but scratches about on the Hun side, quite happy. If he decides to get a Hun, he always gets it because if it runs away he goes right down to the ground after it. Most of his, so far, have been two-seaters. Last week we were easily top of the Brigade with 13 Huns and three balloons.

I got a Fokker biplane out of control. Too misty to see it crash, and too many other Huns about. Saw about six of them dive down right away in the distance, so got onto the back lad without his seeing me. They were attacking a couple of A.W's. We drove the others right out of the sky!

My crowning victory came the other night. I was out on a special job, very late, with Hind and Trubshawe, when to the west I saw archie going like mad. I let fly at full speed and could just make out a machine in the darkness. I cut him off, got behind and below in the orthodox manner, and let blaze. The old boy went straight down for 6,000 feet, and got down to 2,000. I thought he was going to land, but just then old Hind came charging along, and off he started again. I learnt afterwards that I had hit the pilot in the legs. I had a struggle with my guns then, nearly weeping with rage, got them to work again, and both Hind and I shot for all we were worth. The old Hun thought it was no place for him, and landed 1,000 yards our side, just as his machine had started to catch fire. The observer was OK, but pilot badly wounded. As luck would have it the machine was burnt to a cinder, so I was not in luck for souvenirs. However, it isn't everybody's luck to collect a Hun this side. There have only been three since I have been out with the squadron. Unfortunately I am not on speaking terms with most of my friends now, as I am always telling them how to get Huns down this side!![28]

Besides all this nonsense, I have seen a little of the lighter side of life. I met old Mannock on his return to France, and he said, 'Come to a dance in a few days'. I said 'Yes', and duly arrived expecting some show in a hospital. Hanged if I didn't run into the F.A.N.Y. Corps with G – in their midst. As you can imagine I had a most delightful evening. Strangely enough, a few days later I received a memo from Dad, telling me G –'s whereabouts. What a pity I didn't know before.
PS: Bolo (Poler) is home on leave. I told him to call if he felt like it. He shot down a balloon just before he went. He said he hadn't done anything for 'the King and Country', so insisted on doing this!

40 Squadron, RAF. 18 July 1918
My weak little mad self is at last satisfied, and I have got the DFC.[29] I therefore see no reason for staying ·in this dangerous country any longer, and have applied to go home. My application has been duly forwarded, and I shall be surprised if I don't leave this land of strife and arrive at the land of 'hot air' within a week, so don't get nervous if you see me suddenly! I have been offered the *chance* of a squadron at the CFS.

40 Squadron, RAF. 21 July 1918
I am still here but I am on the point of leaving for my homeward journey. I am going home via hospital, so will take a few days. All RAF people go home this way now, for the benefit of some special research work. I knew I could get home any time I liked, as I have been feeling a pretty good physical wreck lately, so I got an MO to examine me, and he stopped me flying.

This is a great squadron, and I am awfully sorry to leave. I have had the happiest times of my life out here, and now that McElroy is back with us, we are easily top squadron in the Brigade. He got a congratulation from General Salmond a few days ago. His Flights are wonderful for great determination and reckless bravery. Five of his Flight found four Huns the other day and mopped up the whole lot! On another day he, and two others, were diving on five Fokker biplanes which were attacking an A.W. and were in turn dived on by six other Fokkers. One of the three stayed behind and drew the six other Fokkers onto him, and succeeded in getting away; while Mac and the other lad shot down three of the original lot. Quite mad, of course! Seven Fokkers attacked Mac and two others a day or two ago, and after a few rounds gave up the fight and cleared! He has now got the DFC too.

Last night I had my farewell dinner. Mick Mannock was there

LEFT: *Fighters from 'Forty' – the author with George McElroy. Between them these two pilots accounted for about 60 enemy aircraft.* RIGHT: *The marker placed on George McElroy's grave at Laventie, 1918.*

with two of his Flight commanders, and also several members of the Brigade. It was a great binge. I feel awfully rotten leaving my priceless Flight. I am awfully pleased that I have had the luck not to lose a single fellow while I have been here, though two went down when I was on leave. Mac I believe thinks it is rather a bad sign, but I am truly thankful! Anyway, before he arrived B Flight led in the number of Huns from the new year. Now I tell Mac that while he counts the number he has shot down, I count the number I see. I believe he is still ahead! He has reached 47 now!!

Captain Gwilym H Lewis, DFC arrived home from France on three weeks' leave, 25 July 1918. At the end of his leave he joined the Central Flying School, Upavon, on 23 August 1918, and continued there until demobilisation, on 28 January 1919.

Lewis was particularly attached to the Central Flying School. On arrival he reported to the Commandant 'Jack' Scott, who was a rare character, and one whom Lewis held in the greatest respect. At this first meeting Scott 'told me that SW area were trying to get me for another job, and that he hoped to put his foot on it'.

Lewis joined the SE5 squadron to become the senior SE5 instructor, and second in command to George (Zulu) Lloyd. Major Jack Slessor was Assistant Commandant at 21 years old, and towards the end of September when Scott was posted to France, he was left in command. It was during this period that a close friendship was formed.

Soon after Lewis's return to England casualties were reported of Keen, 'Shorty' Horsley, McElroy and Hind. The command of 40 Squadron was passed to Compston — 'a very good fellow and they still seem to be doing as well as ever'.

CFS, Upavon, Wiltshire. 20 November 1918
I have excused myself from letter-writing as my dear sister came to see me. As you know, she dived from civilization into this land of 'nowhere-in-particular'. She pounced off the saddle of a bicycle well nigh into my arms, completely disarranging my equilibrium. I had been in a flat spin since Peace Night (of which more anon), trying to bring my fellow instructors and pupils to a state of understanding; my squadron commander being away 'fluing', it rested with me to impress all these beings with what paramount importance it was that they should work twice as hard as they had ever worked before, especially as the war was over, and there was absolutely no point in

Aerial view of the Central Flying School at Upavon, Wiltshire, in 1918.

working! Luckily they had all been in the service long enough to see the sense of my idea, and we were just coming out of our 'spin' when Mary flung herself upon us.

Everything else was in order, so I proceeded to get the sack from the RAF by taking her aloft. She had the unprecedented privilege (?) of being the first she-male to ascend in an SE5, as far as I know. We chased gaily around together, pulled off a loop, a side loop, many stall turns, fully banked turns, and a little contour chase over the ground at something over 110 mph. The lady having acquired a fresh appetite, we side-slipped down to earth and made the best of a good tea. Previous to taking to the atmosphere we had cleverly disguised our passenger as something between a female munition maker and an embryo aviator. However, this was of little avail. The next morning, I had just finished a business-like conversation with one of my sergeants, when he burst out with, 'Excuse me, sir, but please sir, did the lady enjoy her flight?' Of course I hurried to explain it was none other than my sister – and made off with all speed!

I have been very interested in all the glowing accounts of the 11th. I may be a stick in the mud, but Salisbury Plain wasn't muddy enough to stick me on 'Peace Day', or whatever you like to call it. We

A rare two-seat converted SE5A, D3554, at CFS, Upavon, 1918.

got the actual news well on in the morning. It was in no way a shock. It was almost a foregone conclusion, that the business should be signed. However, there was a general feeling that something had got to happen, and in the present flying world that can be easily construed into 'something had got to break'. Some stations proceeded to break everything that would break in their Mess. This was obviously silly, so after firing all the Very lights off at a clown (otherwise known as 'aviator') who flew about in the mist at close range, we bundled off to town. For the time being 'authority' meant nothing to anyone.

We dined in a large party at the RFC Club, and later sallied forth about 20-strong, in formation for the Alhambra. Some stupid patriot had left a large French banner dangling at the end of a large pole, within my reach. I therefore secured this and took up a prominent position in the head of our formation. The population seemed to have turned out in full strength, and a complete atmosphere of general delight seemed to reign. We all felt very pleased with ourselves, and the people generally seemed to be pleased to see us. So during the whole journey we mingled our quite apparent pleasure with much shouting of 'Cheer-O Flying Corps', and such cries as

'Vive La France' (when my banner came in evidence). Some appeared to have been shouting for some considerable time, and not having anything in particular to shout, just shouted.

At certain intervals during our procession down Bond Street and Piccadilly, Very lights were fired aloft with great effect. We managed to secure some sort of permits into the Alhambra, and were again a tremendous success. After rushing about a bit, and having a few little scuffles, during which I lost my hat, we made our way to the front of the dress circle during an interval, and being well to the fore with my banner, and the rest of our party being full of beans and noise, the whole house was soon raised to a complete state of uproar and jubilation. As far as I can remember, I waved my banner over the front of the circle amidst much rejoicing, and shouts of 'We want George (Robey)' and at the same time grasped various people's hats and threw them down at the masses below. By this time the more aristocratic box holders seemed to think that dancing was the most appropriate form of rejoicing, and proceeded to fox-trot round their boxes.

The curtain went up and George Robey appeared with Violet Lorraine amidst shrieks of delight. Whatever they said was completely inaudible, so one of our party threw a tin trumpet onto the stage which Violet proceeded to blow down with considerable vim. However, this only increased the general applause, so she struck up 'Another little drink wouldn't do us any harm', which went down very well. It was then thought time to move on, so I went round to the cloakroom and shouted out a number, in exchange for which I obtained a perfectly good Canadian hat (later taken from me) and got into a very crowded taxi complete 'mit' banner. We caused considerable rejoicing in the Strand, as one of our party stood full length on the roof of the taxi, rather a dangerous performance!

We entered the Savoy with a swing. People were all sitting at their tables concluding their expensive meals. We found another crowd of members of our estimable Service already in the place where the rag-time band ought to have been, so we joined them, many taking up positions of vantage on top of the grand piano. Personally I managed to mount several tables close by, which slowly collapsed under my weight, amidst much crashing of crockery, valiantly waving my banner the while. We rushed about the Savoy in this manner for some time, joining everyone in the general rejoicing.

After that we went for rides in other peoples' taxis, much to the detriment of the taxis, but adding considerably to the gaiety of the nations. I was comfortably perched on one mudguard when to my horror (?) it completely collapsed and I was forced to hurl myself onto the floor of the taxi, much to the delight of the hirers of the taxi (I don't think!) A little fox-trotting in Piccadilly Circus, a passing taxi with two young smart top-hatted young men, driven by an angry driver. Result – one beautiful silk top hat, completely flattened onto owner's head, a lovely feeling! Later return to the Savoy; many good-tempered scuffles; a crash into some people I met at Liverpool. Result, a ripping supper for four of us. And so the most perfect evening went on, and then back to CFS feeling wonderfully fresh and with nothing worse than a black eye!

On returning I had an uncalled for, and quite childish reprimand from the acting Commandant, who for the time being at any rate seemed to have lost all sense of humour. Since then we have continued our training in our usual efficient style, everyone feeling grimly determined not to be found unprepared for the next war. Since Lloyd[30] got the flu I have been running the squadron, at any rate nominally. It has been great fun. One had to be awfully careful with the men, as they are all anxious to quit, and yet a certain standard of discipline must be maintained. If they got thoroughly fed up they might start waving red flags or anything!

Of course, everything has gone wrong, but it has mostly been a case of bad luck. During the last fortnight here there has been a most dreadful epidemic of crashes, and added to that a number of engines have given an unusual amount of trouble. Lloyd is in the RFC Hospital, Eaton Square. All RAF officers and men in London were recalled from leave last Saturday, and no one has been allowed in since. Too much celebrating I suppose.

Notes to Part II

[1] Major Gerald Allen became the first officer commanding No. 112 (Home Defence) Squadron, which was officially formed at Throwley airfield, Essex on 30 July 1917, from a nucleus of personnel and aircraft supplied by No.50 Squadron.

[2] Major Edward Mannock, VC, DSO, MC was killed in action on 26 July 1918. His combat record of 73 accredited victories placed him at the head of the British flying services top-scoring fighter pilots, yet his Victoria Cross was only awarded in July 1919.

[3] Padre B.W. Keymer, the spiritual 'father' of 40 Squadron, 1917-18. After the war he served at RAF Cranwell, 1919-23, where his suggestion for the newly-formed RAF College motto, 'Superna Petimus' (We seek the highest) was officially adopted. He died of pleurisy in 1924, leaving seven children, two of whom were killed in action in the RAF in the 1939-45 war.

[4] Captain J.H. Tudhope, MC, who scored at least eight victories whilst serving with 40 Squadron.

[5] Major Wilfred Ashton McCloughry, MC commanded No.4 Squadron, Australian Flying Corps, which was equipped with Sopwith F.1 Camel scouts. He eventually rose to become Air Commodore, DSO, MC, DFC.

[6] Major James Thomas Byford McCudden, VC, DSO, MC, MM had a remarkable career in the RFC, rising from Air Mechanic in 1913 to Major in 1918. His engineering knowledge, added to an objective analytic approach to air fighting, created new standards in the fighting tactics of the period. His final officially credited score of 57 is thought by many historians to be an underestimation of his true score. McCudden was killed, ironically, in a simple flying accident. On 9 July 1918, flying SE5A,C1126, he was flying to Boffles airfield where he was to assume command of 60 Squadron, but crashed during take-off en route.

[7] William Avery Bishop, VC, DSO, MC, DFC who is generally recognised as the highest-scoring Canadian fighter pilot of 1914-18, being usually credited with 72 victories. During the 1939-45 war he was an Air Marshal in the RCAF; was awarded a CB in 1944, and eventually died peacefully in his sleep on 11 September 1956.

[8] Lieutenant C.O. Rusden who was officially credited with three victories whilst with 40 Squadron.

[9] Captain George Edward Henry McElroy, Dublin-born, was the leading Irish fighter pilot of 1914-18, scoring at least 48 victories during his relatively brief career with Nos 24 and 40 Squadrons. He was killed in action on 31 July 1918, flying SE5A, E1310, and buried by the Germans at Laventie. His prowess was recognised by the awards of two MC's and two DFC's, the latter being gazetted posthumously.

[10] Captain William Leeming Harrison, MC, who was credited with at least 13 victories, mostly with 40 Squadron.

[11] Captain Ian P.R. Napier, MC, who finished the war with a credited 'tally' of 16 victories.

[12] Henry Samson Wolff, who at 5 ft 2 ins was the smallest pilot in 40 Squadron. His lack of inches in no way affected his fighting prowess, being credited with five victories whilst serving with 40 Squadron. Rejoining the RAF in the 1939-45 war, Wolff rose to Wing Commander as a staff officer. He died on 7 June 1972.

[13] Captain Richard James ('Dick') Tipton transferred from the Royal Field Artillery to the RFC in May 1916, and served with 14 Squadron in Egypt. He was shot down on 18 June 1916 and was a prisoner of the Turks for 14 months before managing to escape and return to England. He joined 40 Squadron in France in early 1918, scored one victory on March 6th (Leutnant Walter Conderet of Jagdstaffel 52), but was mortally wounded in combat on March 9th. He succumbed to his wounds three days later.

[14] Lieutenant P La T. Foster was killed in action with Jagdstaffel 52 on 9 March 1918.

[15] Lieutenant R.C. Wade was killed in action on 26 February 1918. Second Lieutenant L.A. Herbert, MM was wounded in action on 24 February 1918, having four confirmed victories during his service with 40 Squadron.

[16] Major Roderic Stanley Dallas, DSC, an Australian, had previously served with No.1 Squadron RNAS, with which unit he had scored a possible total of 43 victories. He was appointed in command of 40 Squadron on 15 March 1918, taking up his appointment on March 17. He then scored a further 12 victories with 40 Squadron before his death in action (See Note 23).

[17] Major-General Sir John Maitland Salmond, who eventually became Marshal of the RAF Sir John Salmond, GCB, CMG, CVO, DSO, DCL, LID. Both Sir John and his brother, ACM Sir Geoffrey Salmond, eventually became Chiefs of the Air Staff – a unique achievement by two brothers in RAF history.

[18] Major-General Sir Frederick Sykes, GCSI, GCIE, GBE, KCB, CMG, who succeeded Major-General Sir Hugh Trenchard as head of the newly-formed Royal Air Force on 15 April 1918.

[19] Rittmeister Manfred Freiherr von Richthofen, Germany's 'Ace of aces' with a credited 80 victories, was killed in combat on 21 April 1918. The RAF officially credited his death to Captain Arthur Roy Brown, DSC, a Canadian serving then with 209 Squadron, but the near-hysterical controversy over the truth of Richthofen's conqueror continues to the present day.

[20] Second Lieutenant W.L. Andrews was brought down in German lines on 15 May 1918, but survived as a prisoner of war.

[21] Lieutenant L. Seymour was shot down on 17 May 1918, but survived as a prisoner of war.

[22] Second Lieutenant G. Watson, credited with two victories, was killed in action on 20 May 1918.

[23] Major Roderic Dallas took off alone in SE5A,D3530, just after 10 am on 1 June 1918. Shortly before mid-day he was engaged by three Fokker Triplanes over Lievin, and Dallas crashed to his death near the road to Bethune, north-west of Lens. He was buried in the British cemetery at Pernes. His conqueror was Leutnant Hans Werner, leader of Jagdstaffel 14 based at Phalempin; Werner's sixth accredited victory.

[24] Lieutenant Don S. Poler, an American, was credited with three confirmed

victories whilst serving with 40 Squadron. He was one of several members of the American Air Service who flew with 40 Squadron; others included Major M.F. Davis, Lieutenants Reed Landis and Paul V. Burwell.

[25] Oberleutnant Kurt Wüsthoff, a 27-victory 'ace', was shot down, wounded, on 17 June 1918 by Lt J.H. Southey of No. 24 Squadron. A prisoner of war, Wüsthoff survived the conflict but, in July 1926, was in an air crash which resulted in both his legs being amputated, and he died later from his severe injuries. A former member of Jagdstaffel 4 of the notorious 'Richthofen Circus', Wüsthoff was serving with Jagdstaffel 15 at the time of his last combat.

[26] A reference to the Fokker D VII single-seater, generally considered to be the finest German fighter to see wide operational service during 1914-18. The first example to reach the fighting front arrived in April 1918, and by July 1 a total of 407 were with operational units. At the time of the Armistice, at least 43 Jagdstaffeln were using the D VII, apart from various second-line units. The D VII's ability to turn at high speed at altitude, combined with its safe stalling characteristics, made it a formidable opponent.

[27] Lieutenant H.W. Clarke, who was wounded in action on 6 July 1918. He was killed in action on 2 September 1918.

[28] This victory was over an LVG CV of Flieger Abteilung Nr.13. The wreckage was designated G/1st Brigade/9 in Allied records, and of its crew Gefreiter Weber became a prisoner. Captain I.F. Hind scored seven confirmed victories before his death in action on 12 August 1918.

[29] The London Gazette citation, dated Air Ministry, 10 Sept, 1918, read: 'Lt /T/Capt- G.H. Lewis (Northampton Regt). It is largely due to this officer's ability and judgement as a Flight leader that many enemy machines have been destroyed with very few casualties in his formation. He is bold in attack, and has personally accounted for eight enemy aircraft, displaying marked disregard of personal danger.' The Distinguished Flying Cross (DFC) was instituted on 3 June 1918 (HM King George V's 53rd birthday) and was to be awarded for achievements 'in the face of the enemy'. Originally the purple and white stripes of the ribbon were horizontal, but in August 1919 these became diagonally placed.

[30] Captain G.L. Lloyd, MC, AFC, known to all in the RFC and RAF as 'Zulu', first served with 60 Squadron in 1917, being awarded his MC for outstanding services in air combat. He was finally credited with a war total of 10 victories.

Demobilised
and
The Second World War

The boy who experienced his first combat when he was eighteen, and as the youngest member of the squadron was given the nickname of 'Cherub', was now a fairly mature man of twenty-one. What then did this new and unknown life hold for this, in some ways, experienced man?

Like so many youngsters before and after me, I had no clue whatever as to what I would like to do. My father had established for himself a prominent position in 'the City'. To me to enter 'the City' was like penetrating into a heavy blank fog. I was offered a job in my father's company at £250 per annum, or there was one in another firm at £200 p.a. I chose the latter. So it happened that I was demobilised on 28 January 1919, and was given a very junior position on January 29 in the great firm of Lloyds Insurance Brokers, Sedgwick, Collins & Company Ltd.

Obviously I was confronted with a complete change of outlook. Of course it had to be a shock – I knew full well that had to be. From being an officer well used to command, and a regular leader into combat of my Flight and sometimes of my squadron, I was relegated to almost the lowest form of office life, and I realised that is where I would have to remain until I learnt the new game. At times it was awfully hard going, as I was under the authority of men for whom I did not have special regard, but there it was. They knew things of which I had no knowledge.

Eventually I was given the opportunity to become one of the firm's brokers at Lloyds, and the good luck which has overshadowed my business career started to take shape. In a few years, I was offered the job of the firm's senior non-marine broker; this was very exciting, but was improbable that it could have happened at such an early date except for the shortage of young men available as a result of the war.

The other side of the coin from the insurance business also embraced a new way of life and was great fun. I joined up with my old Flying Corps pals, Teddy Holstius and Zulu Lloyd, and by sharing living expenses we got along fine. In the summer we rented a small but attractive cottage near the Church at Wargrave on Thames. This we named Tinkerbell. Every Sunday morning Zulu and I would be battling with two bachelor friends owning the finest grasscourts you could find, having most likely played cricket with the village on the previous Saturday afternoon. Teddy was one of those good looking humorous extroverts, liked and enjoyed by everyone. I think I would not be far wrong in comparing him to David Niven. He was friendly with Noel Coward, and many were the occasions when on a Saturday night, we would be disturbed by noises outside our cottage and Noel would be there, and as often as not with his friend Betty Chester. I remember the Sunday morning when we lay in our punt and Noel read to us his first play, *The Rat Trap*. I do not recall if it was ever staged. At that point Noel was at the beginning, and was inclined to be rather anti-social in the sense that in his plays he liked to poke fun at the Hunting Set or the Establishment. Of course this all changed later on.

In the winter we would go back to London. In the evening oftimes we were at deb dances, immaculately dressed in white ties and toppers, but never failing to ask our elderly hostesses to dance, and to say our thanks, a practice which now seems to be very 'old hat'. Indeed, those days immediately following the war were for us in many ways great fun.

By this time I was wedded to my job. Sedgwick Collins was tops and I loved the firm. Wherever I could wave the flag I did so enthusiastically. Further to that Lloyds held my interest and fascination. In 1923, I was sent to America, and on my return I was allowed to form a new 'American non-marine department' which I did with a staff of three. At about the same time I was appointed a full Director of the Firm, although admittedly a very junior one. With luck and a little judgement the Department remained virtually unscathed after the market crashed in 1929. The American marine side however encountered some serious problems.

In 1925, I was married to Christian Robertson, as Scotch as I am Welsh. She threw herself wholeheartedly into giving all the support she could, whether on exhausting business trips, or at home, and without this unstinted backing such success as I have enjoyed simply would not have been possible. On top of it all, she was mainly responsible for bringing up three pretty nice children.

By the time the Second World War was looming up, the American non-marine department had of course expanded considerably, and had outstripped all other departments in brokerage volumes and certainly in profit. But about the middle of 1938, I had a surprise phone call from Jack Slessor. Would I please come and have a drink? War was in the air – it may well have been shortly before the surrender of Munich in September, but following the rape of Austria in March. During the year we had taken a new house near Regent's Park, and I decided then to build a substantial concrete shelter in the garden. I met Jack Slessor in his flat – at that time he was head of the Plans branch of the Air Staff. With him was Wilfred Freeman – as I recall later, Air Chief Marshal Sir Wilfred Freeman, Air Member for Development and Production, and in 1940, Vice Chief of the Air Staff, Jack Slessor told me that they were planning a 'joint service' operation and a War Room available to the Prime Minister and the War Cabinet. Basically I recall he said they did not want any more 'Lloyd George breakfasts', and they wanted some 'chaps' to keep the situation under control. I was asked if I would be one of the Air Force Officers. I questioned him on the 'Joint' Service side, as that meant a great deal to me. Before the first war, as I understood it, the Services made their own arrangements with industry. On the battle front we were terribly hard pressed for good aero engines, particularly during the SE5A and Dolphin period, and I understood that the Navy had the sole contract with Rolls Royce, which made me boil with fury. I considered the fine performance of the Fokker D.VII's was almost entirely due to the reliability and high performance of their Mercedes and BMW engines. A Joint Service attitude meant a great deal to me, so apart from the compliment I was anxious to accept, even though I was very much lacking in Service qualifications. I was nearing 43. I had only a vague idea what the job would be. Definitely I felt too old to fly again but of course when you get into uniform you do just what you are told.

Clearly the Joint Planning Staffs had already planned for this as the 'Central War Room' from which we were to operate was already prepared in the basement of Storey's Gate, not far from Downing Street, together with the necessary accommodation for War Cabinet, Chiefs of Staff and the Central Operational and Intelligence staff bodies.

We were asked to 'man' this War Room as civilians, and we reported to the Directorate of Plans. In due course I met the officers in the other services. There were four of us in each section. In the RAF we were mostly pilots who had flown in the World War I but since had assumed responsible civilian jobs. The representatives of other two services were or had been regular officers. For a year or more before the outbreak of war, our custom was to meet in the evenings, and display on the maps mostly the disposition of the German forces, and assemble the various orders of Battle for Army, Navy and Air – German, French and our own. The limitations of the British war equipment was pitiful – not enough machine guns even to spare one for a merchant ship. But when we displayed the dispositions of the German Forces in or around Austria and Czechoslovakia, the situation was so utterly revealing that we felt the members of the Cabinet must surely be able to grasp it. It is generally accepted that we should have recognised what we were up against when Austria was swallowed up. Politically we did not do so until after the rape of Czechoslovakia in March 1939 – and even then we did not get down to arming ourselves in the necessary scale and tempo until after the fall of France in 1940.

Our meetings were of course secret, and when we were shown the future plans of the Air Force at the outbreak of war, it became clear that we would be operating in a very confidential area.

That year or more in the Central War Room was concerned with great activity in the outer world, and from our view point, was especially interesting. In March 1938 came Hitler's invasion of Austria. The surrender at München in September, the final overwhelming of Czechoslovakia in March 1939. To the ordinary man not in a position to be aware of the thoughts and pressures that influenced the minds of the Government and their military advisers in the years before September 1939, it did appear as if the Government was quite frighteningly inept and prone to appeasement.

In the event, as a result of Chamberlain's 'Peace in our Time' talks with Hitler, we had a year in which to prepare and pull ourselves together and re-equip. There will be diverse opinions as to whether it would have been advantageous to take action in 1938 or not. Probably the crux of the matter lies in the confidence felt in the French Forces. From some of us with experience of the 1914/18 period, that feeling of confidence was not strong.

Without doubt the air power of the Royal Air Force was seriously or terrifyingly weak in relation to the German Air Force. We were extremely fortunate in having at the head of the Air Staff such brilliant officers as Jack Slessor, later CAS, and Marshal of the Royal Air Force, Sir John Slessor; Wilfred Freeman, later Air Chief Marshal Sir Wilfred Freeman; the CAS Sir Cyril Newall, later Marshal of the Royal Air Force the Lord Newall; and Sir Charles Portal, later CAS and Marshal of the Royal Air Force, the Lord Portal.

Decisions were made prior to the outbreak of war which lead to the production of a Fighter Command force of sufficient strength and quality of aircraft to win the Battle of Britain, and probably saved us from early defeat. The bomber side took longer to reach fruition, but the Air Staff had decided that our striking force should be equipped with the heavy four engined type bomber, far exceeding in power anything the Germans had in any quantity. Together with the United States Air Force, there can be no doubt that this represented a true requirement for victory.

We were finally called up a week before the outbreak of hostilities. There had been some question of what rank we should be given – it was considered it had to be adequate to exert some degree of authority. So we were all made the equivalent of Lieut.Colonels which for us it was Wing Commanders in the RAF Volunteer Reserve. For some time we wore a 'VR' on our collars.

I put it to my Chairman, Aynsley Greenwell, asking him what would be my position in the circumstances. My colleagues were as generous to me as I could possibly have hoped. My wife and family had remained in Anglesey where I had inherited a sea-side holiday house built by my parents.

I think it may have been on the first day of the war, that we heard in London the dreary wail of the air raid siren. It was a false alarm, but a precursor of the warning of danger to which Londoners were to become very familiar indeed.

The War Room was manned by the three services throughout the 24 hours, each showing a roster for the night shifts. When off duty if air raids became particularly tiresome, we would throw a mattress on the floor, but that didn't happen very often. For transportation in day time the buses were running well, and at night I would oftimes use a push bicycle, but London was a very dark place indeed.

As the war progressed, I found our work fascinatingly interesting.

We were attached to the Directorate of Plans of our respective services. The various rooms bordering on our main underground passageway operated under the Commandant Captain Adams, RN, the civilian representative was Mr Rance and the defence of the area was the responsibility of the Royal Marines, and a very helpful lot they were. Considerable thought had been given to reinforcing the whole structure against bombing, providing air conditioning and alternative systems of lighting, etc. This basement subsequently became the citadel of Whitehall.

Our operations were essentially for the benefit of the planning staffs of the Prime Minister, the War Cabinet, the Chiefs of Staff, and indeed the Monarch. Despite our attachment to the Directorate of Plans, we had nothing whatever to do with the conduct of the war, but were responsible for the reporting of events as they occurred, and for the maintenance of strategic maps of the various theatres of war.

A variety of officers of all services and of the required status, would

The Cabinet War Room, circa 1944. Personnel identified are, from right: Wg Cdr Rees; Wg Cdr John J Heagerty; Cmdr Bosanquet, R.N. The two officers studying the wall map were from the Joint Planners Section.

be interested in, or partially responsible for the War Room activities. What struck me in short order was the capabilities and high intelligence of many of these men. Maybe I was a bit cocky coming from the world of keenness and competition, but very soon my thoughts were on how extremely valuable many of these men would be in my realm of activity. Essentially they were from the planning staff of the three services. A delightful sparkling humorous character was Wing Commander W.F. Dickson. As I recall he took charge of the War Room to steer us on the right lines – certainly he took charge of the RAF section. It wasn't too long before he left us on promotion, only to finish up after the War as Air Marshal Sir William Dickson, GCB, KBE, DSO, AFC, Chief of the Air Staff and Chairman of the Combined Chiefs of Staff Committee. Another very able character who helped to steer our operations in the early stages was Hugh Fraser, who also was to become an Air Vice Marshal. A deputy to Slessor, and very sound and very able. Certainly he was a complete master hand at drafting a report. On occasions he accompanied Slessor on visits to General Gamelin and to other French Staff meetings. I think that at that time Slessor's personal opinion of Gamelin was not very favourable – that he was a courtly and confident old soldier but quite unequal to the job.

Another Air Force visitor whose friendly sparkle we enjoyed very much was Dermot Boyle (later CAS Marshal of the Royal Air Force Sir Dermot Boyle). Earlier on he was an outstanding pilot and instructor at the Central Flying School and one of the earliest graduates of the RAF College at Cranwell. Everyone in our area appeared to work on a Joint Service basis, the joint planners were similarly constituted and of course we were ourselves.

Our main functions were to prepare each morning (normally by 6 a.m.) a brief summary of what had happened in the previous 24 hours. Each service contributed its section and seldom would the whole extend over one foolscap sheet of paper. This was typed and available for the Chiefs of Staff and the Prime Minister at their 8 a.m. meeting. Brevity and accuracy was what they required. On occasions at the start I found it difficult not to go into a little detail on some exploits of the RAF. On one such occasion Mr Churchill returned the paper with the comments: 'No trench raids please'! which I thought was very apposite. Another copy we took each morning to Buckingham Palace and left it with the Monarch's secretary, enlarging on any details that he considered might be of special interest. It was quite a little sensation to be waved on through the main gates by the Palace police guard.

At the end of each week we prepared a more detailed resume which was circulated to the members of the War Cabinet, and I was many times told it was found highly acceptable.

On the wall space of the War Room were placed maps covering various theatres of the war. At the top end covering the whole wall was the naval world wide map with the Atlantic Ocean in the centre. On this were plotted the various Atlantic, Archangel, Gibraltar, convoys and their sinkings, and other matters of naval importance. The Navy always with their high regard for security were never too keen even for their War Room colleagues to spend too much time browsing over the dispositions of their ships and convoys.

The Army of course showed details of the Western Front when there was one, the Desert, the dispositions of our own and enemy Corps during and after the Normandy landings. What was of particular interest was the Russian front, and this proved especially so for those commanders from overseas, who had a right of entry to the War Room.

Our forces mobilised on 1 September 1939, the day the Germans at last invaded Poland. Many months were to pass before we were seriously attacked. Poland was overwhelmed far more easily and quickly than anyone had thought possible by the *Blitzkrieg*.

For some months after that was the unreality of the 'phoney war'. We made gallantly fought combined operations on Narvik with a plan to cut off the iron-ore supplies to Germany, and another at Trondheim, but we were forced to withdraw. All the while the German armies were silently concentrating in the Rhineland and the Luftwaffe building up for the grand assault against England which was to follow the conquest of France.

The information received over the secret scrambler telephones of our three services was relayed briefly to the Chiefs of Staff. It was made quite clear to us that it would have to be an exceptional message which would warrant our disturbing the Prime Minister. His hours for rest were his own affair. However, on 10 May 1940, at about 2 a.m. I received a signal through our RAF channels that the Germans had invaded Holland. I decided that the Prime Minister should be advised, and instructed his PA accordingly. In the event, I must have been justified, as the Chiefs of Staff were alerted and met at 6 a.m. We thought we knew about everything that was going on, but now I know we did not, as we were not in the picture regarding the 'Ultra Secret'*. With the benefit of this source of information it is possible the PM would have been already alerted before the Germans attacked.

Ten days later after the German break through in the Ardennes, the situation in France was desperately dangerous and Lord Gort had to consider the possibility of a withdrawal of the BEF towards the coast.

After the collapse of the French Army came the miracle of the evacuation from Dunkirk which brought 340,000 men away. During the Battle of France and the withdrawal from Dunkirk the RAF lost nearly 1000 aircraft. By June 14 Europe had been completely overrun. In Sir John Slessor's book *The Central Blue* (Cassell, 1956) he wrote as follows:

> It was a grim moment when on June 14th a meeting of the Joint Planning Committee was interrupted by Wing Commander G.H. Lewis, a duty officer at the Cabinet War Room, with a laconic message from our liaison mission with General Georges: 'Organised resistance in France is at an end'. But the prevailing sensation in the neon-lighted room under the War Cabinet Office was one of relief – a feeling that at last we knew the worst, and our salvation now depended on ourselves alone.

> In messages of this sort history was passing before ones eyes in the War Room. This became clearer to me later when Jack Slessor invited me to visit him when he commanded No. 5 Group of Bomber Command and there on the wall of his office hung this message contained in a small frame, but I regret shamefully badly written in red chalk!

I have no intention of writing a history of the war. But at this stage we were in an intensely grim situation, in which we now found ourselves alone, and confronted by our enemy who was in possession of the whole coast line from the North Cape to the Bay of Biscay, and the Luftwaffe concentrating for the knock-out blow.

During these months of the war I had a feeling of strain – not very surprising considering our lack of preparation before the War, but all the time there was one piece of bad news after another – when we were for ever stopping up holes, and when our entire expeditionary force appeared to be in hopeless plight, in my inside, I became really

* By means of this secret we were able to decode the signals passed from Hitler's HQ to his commanders in the field and vice-versa.

concerned. Nothing to do with Hitler. I didn't care a damn about him. Certainly nothing to do with the War Room or the joint planners, all of whom felt in their bones that we could not be defeated.

During this period I do not ever recall a rush of visitors, but rather fairly isolated individuals. Some of the War Cabinet would come along, but not all of them. Eden and Lyttelton quite often, and even more frequently, Major Clem Atlee, who had served in the first war. In his rather shy manner he quite liked to join us for the odd drink in our little sub-basement mess. Mostly the Ministers' faces showed their anxiety, and I felt it was up to me to cheer them up, as they browsed from one map to the other. I do not ever remember seeing Mr Chamberlain. Mr Churchill was more inclined to be around in the early morning, about 7 a.m., in his siren suit. In his gruff way, he shot quick questions and liked clear answers, but he was always courteous and polite.

And then from the centre of this gloom and anxiety, we would hear our Prime Minister making a fantastic rousing speech to the nation, broadcasting from his small unpretentious office and bed room almost next door to the War Room. 'We will fight on the beaches', and 'Blood and Sweat' and all the rest. The worse the conditions became, the more his invincible spirit would rise and proved an immense moral tonic for our people. He would leave Hitler guessing, at the same time by wrapping up his statements in his inimitable phrases; he never uttered a sentence that was not strictly true.

Then came the German Air 'Blitz' concentrated on our airfields, and then to a large measure on London. London was a marvellous place – only the people who needed to remained; the rest cleared out for one reason or another. At the heart of it were those real London cockneys, quick, gay, humorous and full of guts. The bombing was very serious indeed – it was difficult to find a single London square that had not been seriously hit, perhaps several times, and there was the very serious raid on the City in the area of St. Pauls, and the great difficulty in putting out the fires before the night to follow. The civilians were involved in a variety of services only to mention the magnificent body of air raid wardens, and those fire fighters manning roof tops throughout the night. In fact everyone had their stirrup pump and their buckets of sand to deal with the 'incendiaries'.

My own family was away, so I was able to house three or four fellow officers and also my sister-in-law, Maisie Robertson, who became quite a key person in MO1. They slept in the basement, and I mostly slept in my shelter. In those days, we had a cook, and young Lilian, a good one, decided to stay with us. I fixed her up with an Anderson shelter on the floor of her sitting room which was on terra firma, and each night she crept into this, and she was quite frightened. The theory was that the bomb which was a direct hit you didn't hear coming. I do not know who proved this. One raid I heard a big one fizzing down from thousands of feet, and I thought it was mine. In the event, it fell the other side of a wall about fifteen yards away, lifted me and my concrete shelter upwards, threw some solid lumps of London clay so high that on returning to earth penetrated the roof of the house, and of course shattered all the windows on that side. The others were sleeping in the basement on the other side of the house, and I chided them as they hadn't bothered to have a look to see how it was with me. But they didn't, and that is how it was. In fact it was a bad raid, and the Huns really blasted the Marylebone marshalling yards, to the extent that where I was a mile away the fires were such that I could read the paper and the birds started up their dawn chorus!

But Fighter Command now equipped with their Spitfires and Hurricanes proved a match for the German Luftwaffe and Hitler abandoned his invasion. Control of the air was an essential for his operation. Churchill's comment was: 'Never did so many owe so much to so few'. In the War Room on 15 September 1940, we showed: Destroyed 183; Probable 42; Damaged 75. Our own 28. This proved to be an exaggeration, but that did not really matter. It can easily happen in dog fights when two aircraft may attack the same enemy. No doubt at all that at the end of the day, the Germans had a very unserviceable air force. Certainly Hitler had had enough.

And so from 1939 to 1945 the European war progressed and the bad news turned to good news – the Americans were attacked at Pearl Harbour by the foolhardy Japs and Germany declared war on America. This indeed was one of Churchill's finest hours, as indeed it was for the Allies. Another outstanding event of good news was the victory of the 8th Army under General Montgomery at Alamein. That really cheered everyone up, and not least in the War Room and amongst the Joint Planners.

The German Navy continued with her battle of the Atlantic with unabated violence. The sinkings of British Allied and neutral shipping by her 'U' boats reached a crucial level. In 1942, losses had reached the staggering total of nearly 8,000,000 gross tons – disastrously more than the rate of new construction. An all out effort had to be made by the Allies, and by the end of 1943, it can be said with reasonable certainty that about 284 U-boats (including Italian and Japanese) were destroyed. It is not always appreciated the considerable contribution that was provided by Coastal Command with the US Squadrons operating under our operational control and commanded by Sir John Slessor. About 93 of the total were sunk by surface ships and 126 by shore-based aircraft, of which 87 were credited to Coastal Command.

During the whole year only one ship was sunk when air escort was actually present. These comments are in no way a reflection on the marvellous job performed by the Navy. In any event, there was a limit to the range of Coastal Command's very long range aircraft. But it is of interest in assessing this contribution to the air offensive. 1943 saw the defeat of the U-boat menace in the Atlantic.

Of the various Directors of Plans under whom we served, a trio who made a very real impression on me were Air Commodore William Elliot, Captain Charles Lambe, and Colonel Guy Stewart. One would have to go far to find three more able officers. Bill Elliot was personally a delightful person, particularly in so far as our own RAF section was concerned.

And so the war continued in its day to day struggle and variety. For the War Room our basic duties were virtually unaltered, but at all times fundamentally interesting. I do not know what went wrong with me but I began to suffer from duodenal bothers, and for a time I was hospitalised, and given sick leave. When I returned, the MO said I was not to do night duty. With unbelievably good nature my other colleagues decided they would assume my night duty for me. Some time later I was given a Medical Board, and invalided out in the last year of the European War. By this time our American and Russian Allies were in to help in a very big way indeed. The heavy bombers for Bomber Command that Wilfrid Freeman programmed in 1938 waded in with great power and effect. Together with the American bomber force the Germans were vitally softened up both militarily and economically. Our return to Europe alongside our American allies and the joint service operation of the landing on the Normandy beaches was one of the most imaginative and brilliant operations ever performed in war.

Two officers who particularly remain in my mind – General 'Pug' Ismay and General Ian Jacobs. Jacobs, I presume, lost out to some extent as he was unable to get away and command an operational unit. A brilliant staff officer, and at all times ready to enlarge on a situation to us in proper military terms. 'Pug' Ismay knew everyone in the War Room, and was always ready to spin a yarn or enjoy a joke.

That was the end of my time with the Royal Air Force. In London all that was left to us were the 'Doodlebugs' and the V2's. These latter rockets were very unpleasant and could have caused much trouble if they had arrived earlier in numbers. The 'doodlebugs' at night could be sinister. They had a habit of flying right over my house at about 300 ft, showing their flare path down the garden. In the quiet of night, one heard their approach miles away – then as they came louder and closer and closer, so ones apprehension would increase. At that point all that mattered was that the engine would keep going – if not! – well I never had that experience at such close quarters. In all, our windows were blown in five times.

Jack Slessor, who as Director of Plans was responsible for my service in the Cabinet War Room, continued to contribute to the war effort on a very high level. He took part in many of our most important conferences with French, American and Allied Generals, including a fire side chat with Roosevelt, in Washington, before America had entered the war. From the Air Ministry, he took command in 1941-2 of No. 5 Bomber Group. He then was the very effective Commander in Chief of Coastal Command, and finally took over from Air Chief Marshal Sir Arthur Tedder, the Command of the RAF in the Mediterranean and Middle East. Finally, this young Major, who in 1918, at the age of 21 or 22, became acting Commandant of the great training centre, the Central Flying School, completed his service career as Chief of the Air Staff, Marshal of the Royal Air Force, Sir John Slessor, GCB, DSO, MC.

Certainly there are no heroics in this chapter. I put away the uniform of the flying services I had been so proud to wear, for about ten years, for the last time. Thirty years had passed since the days of the 35 HP Caudron to the days of the mighty aircraft which now were perhaps the decisive factor in the greatest war in history.

During the whole period of the War, I had received all office cables exchanged by the American non-marine department. I was able to take up my bowler hat again more or less where I had left off. But in a couple of years, need I say, to my great surprise, I was out of a job. Businesswise the American non-marine department had expanded from a staff of three to about forty five – the brokerage earned in the department had exceeded that of any department in the office – I had never asked for a rise in salary, but my colleagues had voted me the largest share of the profits of any director, including the Chairman. Amongst other items, through my father's influence, I had introduced the very valuable New India Insurance Company reinsurance account, and indeed, I was much pleased to have added to the Marine side by bringing in the China Steam Navigation Fleet, and to have formed an Aviation Section under John Roscoe. It is true that the composition of the Board had changed considerably during these five years, and there was a new Chairman. I mention this because it was a sidelight on commercial life which in a strange sort of way fascinated me. The fact of the matter is of course that to be away from the office for five years was too long and that was that. It was not my intention however after 25 years hard going as a director, without a row with anyone, or having robbed the till, that I should disappear from the scene quite like that!

I was at this point over 50 years of age – all rather awkward. Christian said, as I well recall, 'Now is the time to do something worth while with your life.' I agreed, and tried hard. I became very busy, but really I was getting nowhere. Quite truly my heart was at Lloyds.

One day an old friend, a leading Marine Underwriter, and a member of the committee of Lloyds, Tony Gale, said, 'Why don't you have a talk with Henry Booker?' He was Chairman of a smallish but old established firm of Lloyds Brokers called Arbon Langrish & Co. In business he was quite a thruster, and a very able marine broker. By the start of 1951 we had made a deal. I didn't want another boss, so we agreed to be joint managing directors on a fifty-fifty basis. I found myself back at square one, having to produce business on the American side, and in a measure to go into the market and place it. It is tough going to work up new business which in any event needs time to take shape and settle down. However, quite soon the business started to pour in, and the American department again became the most profitable unit of the office. But in 1953 a very sad thing happened in the sudden death of Henry Booker. I was now Chairman of the whole organisation. I remember

Golden Wedding. Gwilym Hugh Lewis and his wife, Christian – a photo taken to celebrate their golden wedding anniversary in July 1975.

going on my knees and praying for wisdom.

We became a happy firm and I gathered a strong team round me. The business progressed dramatically. In 1965 the firm was merged with Clarksons as a result of which we all greatly benefitted materially.

At the end of 1974 I finally hauled down my flag and my colleagues gave Christian and myself a wonderful farewell party.

It was very much in my mind in my early days that my contribution was to build and create something which would continue after me. I am not sure that I accomplished that. My work was my pleasure and my pleasure was my work. Clearly I had enjoyed incredibly good luck, and after giving me one severe check the Almighty allowed me to progress again. My attachment to Lloyds is deep seated and sincere. It was part of my good fortune that that was where I was to work – a very democratic institution where people expand in keen competition and where decency and honesty override all business standards. Furthermore there is a risk element but profit is by no means a 'dirty' word and a considerable contribution to Britain's overseas earnings is the result of individual enterprise and much self sacrifice.

I do not feel I have deserved such good fortune, but that is how it has been since the early days of the boy of eighteen when by all the rules he should have been shot down in the very first encounter with a Roland 2-seater. Without such marvellous backing up from Christian it must have been a very different story. We are happy to have just celebrated our Golden Wedding. Looking back over the whole shooting match it has all been the greatest of fun.

INDEX

(Places and Names)